ANXIETY

Using Science to Rewire Your Anxious Brain

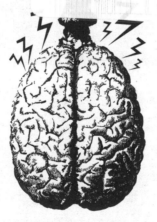

FAITH G. HARPER, PhD, LPC-S, ACS, ACN

Microcosm Publishing
Portland, OR

UNF#CK YOUR ANXIETY
Using Science to Rewire Your Anxious Brain

Part of the 5 Minute Therapy Series
© Dr. Faith Harper, 2016, 2018, 2021
This edition © Microcosm Publishing, 2021
First edition, first published 2016
Third edition, first published March 9, 2021

For a catalog, write or visit:
Microcosm Publishing
2752 N Williams Ave.
Portland, OR 97227
www.Microcosm.Pub

ISBN 978-1-62106-548-7
This is Microcosm #205
Edited by Lydia Rogue
Design by Joe Biel

To join the ranks of high-class stores that feature Microcosm titles, talk to your local rep: In the U.S. **Como** (Atlantic), **Fujii** (Midwest), **Travelers West** (Pacific), **Brunswick** in Canada, **Turnaround** in Europe, **New South** in Australia and New Zealand, and **Baker & Taylor Publisher Services** in Asia, India, and South Africa. We are sold in the gift market by **Gifts of Nature** and by **Faire**.

Global labor conditions are bad, and our roots in industrial Cleveland in the 70s and 80s made us appreciate the need to treat workers right. Therefore, our books are MADE IN THE USA.

Library of Congress Cataloging-in-Publication Data

Names: Harper, Faith G., author.
Title: Unfuck your anxiety : using science to rewrite your anxious brain /
    Faith G. Harper, PhD, LPC-S, ACS, ACN.
Other titles: This is your brain on anxiety
Description: [2nd edition]. | Portland : Microcosm Publishing, [2021] |
    Revision of: This is your brain on anxiety. 2018. | Summary: "Anxiety is
    a survival skill gone haywire. It happens when our brain is working so
    hard to protect us that it forgets to notice that the danger has passed.
    It feels like choking, stifling, smothering, tingling, panicking-our
    brains cut out and we start to make bad decisions-all normal anxiety
    reactions. Dr. Faith G. Harper, author of the bestselling Unfuck Your
    Brain and This is Your Brain on Depression, packs a ton of knowledge and
    help into this practical manual. She helps us understand the history and
    science of anxiety, realize when it's become a serious problem, know the
    difference between anxiety and other conditions, and cope with it in the
    moment as well as addressing it long term. This updated-and-expanded
    book is a lifesaver for panic attacks, breaking out of
    flight-fight-freeze responses, similar and co-occurring conditions, and
    for chronic anxiety. Straightforward, funny, kind, and judgment free, it
    includes a wide range of tips, exercises, and medical interventions.
    It's also good for people who aren't burdened by daily anxiety but want
    to cope better with the tough life situations we all face. Read this
    book and breathe!"-- Provided by publisher.
Identifiers: LCCN 2021004686 | ISBN 9781621065487 (paperback)
Subjects: LCSH: Anxiety disorders. | Anxiety disorders--Treatment.
Classification: LCC RC531 .H37 2021 | DDC 616.85/22--dc23
LC record available at https://lccn.loc.gov/2021004686

MICROCOSM·PUBLISHING

Microcosm Publishing is Portland's most diversified publishing house and distributor with a focus on the colorful, authentic, and empowering. Our books and zines have put your power in your hands since 1996, equipping readers to make positive changes in their lives and in the world around them. Microcosm emphasizes skill-building, showing hidden histories, and fostering creativity through challenging conventional publishing wisdom with books and bookettes about DIY skills, food, bicycling, gender, self-care, and social justice. What was once a distro and record label was started by Joe Biel in his bedroom and has become among the oldest independent publishing houses in Portland, OR. We are a politically moderate, centrist publisher in a world that has inched to the right for the past 80 years.

Did you know that you can buy our books directly from us at sliding scale rates? Support a small, independent publisher and pay less than Amazon's price at **www.Microcosm.Pub**

CONTENTS

NEW
INTRODUCTION

Anyone with anxiety would fail a lie detector test over it.

"Stop being anxious" has never worked in the history of ever, has it? Someone telling you not to be anxious has never netted the response of *"Holy shit, I never thought of that! I'm totally good now, thanks Big Daddy!"*

Expecting you to just suppress your anxiety is ridiculous. I mean, you can *say* you're fine but if you were hooked up to a lie detector your body would be screaming bloody murder that you are clearly as unfine as fuck. Which means if we can see the numbers we need to treat it as the very real health issue/public health crisis that it is.

Which leads me to why this book came to be.

The original version of this book, *This Is Your Brain On Anxiety*, did better than probably everyone expected it to. Or at least better than I expected it to. I imagine that the inescapable reality of chaos politics, pandemics, and deep state racism helped sales. Unfortunately. But even current reality aside, anxiety is a common and universal human experience with some great books written about it and a ton of really awful ones.

People kept reaching out to me saying *"Holy shit, I got so much more from this tiny book than all these other door-stop sized books!"* which is admittedly great for my ego, but a depressing commentary on the utility of what else is out there.

So that got us to thinking . . . could we bump up our game? Could we expand the anxiety book with just enough stuff to make it more useful without making it a fifty dollar doorstop?

And? Fuck, yeah, we can do that.

So that's what we did here. I included a lot more information about different types of anxiety disorders, more specifics on treatment options, more DIY anxiety management tools, and even more science on brain differences and cultural differences that lend themselves to anxiety. Cuz y'all my fellow nerds and I love it.

(Not to mention the fact that there are some *amazing* books out there on anxiety so I expanded my list of favorites in the appendix. None are 50 dollar doorstops. All are incredibly useful and/or incredible context regarding the human condition.)

Original Introduction

When you struggle with anxiety, the most empowering thing in the world is realizing that you aren't weak, broken, or batshit crazy.

I'm not just saying that to placate you. It's scientifically true. Anxiety makes perfect sense because it's how our brains are wired to protect us. Certain mental health issues, anxiety being one of them, are the direct result of how we have evolved for survival. Certain memories are stored in certain ways in order to protect you. When those memories are triggered, rational thought gets bypassed and your body goes into *do something to fix this* mode. (If you wanna nerd out more on the brain science stuff, you should totally read my other book, *Unfuck Your Brain.*)

If you're still reading, that probably means that your brain regularly gets hijacked by anxiety. And you're over that shit. And you want your life back. So here's what we're going to talk about:

1) What anxiety actually is. You know, as opposed to all those other emotional states (fear, depression, etc.) that seem all vaguely interconnected but have a lot of differences in terms of what's going on in the brain and how we can best manage them.

2) The whole brain science/brain chemistry aspect of how anxiety is triggered.

3) The how-to-deal-with-it part. Both in the middle of an attack, and more generally over the long term.

4) How to cope when you also have to deal with other people, relationships, jobs, schools, etc. Anxiety wouldn't be so bad if it wasn't for other people in your life, right?

5) How to provide support if someone you care about has anxiety. Because that's just as helpless a feeling as having anxiety yourself.

Has anyone ever told you "You should try yoga! Or meditation! Or keep a thought diary! Or spin in a circle three times when a bell rings!"

Sometimes (okay, a lot of times) people will suggest something because they read about it, or tried it themselves, or saw other people try it and that it helped. But when you're in the midst of feeling anxious, you look at any option and think, can this actually help my anxiety? And if so, how is it actually helping?

We all get to a point where we are tired of spinning around when the bells ring in hopes of feeling better.

So along with the "this is the why shit's fucked" portion of the book, I'll explain the why part again with the fixing it part. Like "this is helpful because it counteracts this chemical in your body with this other one" or "this is helpful because it helps unpack thinking habits that tend to reinforce anxiety and we're gonna try to break that cycle."

Seeking the rationale behind whatever I'm doing, or working with clients to do, has made me a better therapist. It's definitely made me a healthier person. We should never swallow everything we're told as absolute truth. So, I did my research, figured out why things worked, and figured out ways sometimes to make them work better. That's how this book came into existence.

If you are nodding your head in agreement? You're gonna get as much out of reading it as I did out of writing it.

THIS IS YOUR BRAIN ON ANXIETY

What is Anxiety?

The American Psychological Association defines anxiety as *"an emotion characterized by feelings of tension, worried thoughts and physical changes like increased blood pressure."* Maybe a diagnostic starting point, but still undersells the carnival fun house that anxiety really is, so let's go a little deeper, yeah?

Anxiety is a human condition that we have been grappling with for centuries. To be sure, modern living is stressful as hell. But modern life is not the source of human anxiety. Humanity in and of itself is an anxiety-provoking experience for so many people. The formal "name it and claim it" process of recognizing human anxiety didn't come until much later,

Psychologist Rollo May's work as an existential therapist[1] in the middle part of the 20th century focused substantially on the problem of human anxiety. He didn't have Google

---

1 Existential therapists focused on life fuckery through a philosophical lens, sort of aiming to understand our higher selves rather than just consider us the sum total of our behaviors.

algorithms to tell him the word popped up in the 19th century and has been a thing ever since. But he was a fucking brilliant scholar of philosophy, and his understanding of human anxiety was largely based in his readings of the humanistic philosophers such as Bertrand Russell.

A major philosophical shift in how humans viewed themselves started in the 19th century. This was a movement towards technical reason: the idea that our best decision-making occurs when we are detached from our emotional reactions. This was a new thing. In the 17th century, the big philosophical idea was one of *rational reason*: the belief that emotions are a source of information about the situations we encounter, although they shouldn't be the presiding force in our decision making processes. Technical reason, on the other hand, suggests that emotions have *no* place in decision-making at all. Instead of honoring the existence of emotions, people came to believe we should repress them.

So as Rollo May oh so dryly noted in his book *The Meaning of Anxiety*, originally published in 1950: *"In view of this psychological disunity, it is not surprising that anxiety should have emerged as an unavoidable problem in the nineteenth century."*

May's book continues to be in print decades later as it still stands as an accurate representation of anxiety as an integral part of the human condition. It is something to live with and learn from, rather than something to suppress and eradicate. This means he believed that reason is not the source of meaning. And that meaning-making in general cannot be universalized but is something unique within each of us. May invoked Kierkegaard's belief that our true vocation in life is to be our unique selves. So it makes sense that anxiety occurs when we perceive possible danger around us. And that danger often includes how being our unique selves is denied to us on such a huge cultural level.

I think there is a lot of truth there. *But*. There is more to it than that.

The whole field of psychology is based on the worldviews of European and European-American men with significant educational privilege and at least some level of financial privilege.

Being an educated white guy is by no means a background that protects you from anxiety, but you may experience anxiety in a different way than most other people. If you are an academic or researcher, your background will also shape how you theorize what anxiety is and how to manage it.

In the 1970s, there was a pretty huge shift in the theoretical work of mental and emotional health. Something we now call Relational Cultural Theory (RCT) started being written about and talked about by women in academia. The theorists central to RCT (e.g. Jean Baker Miller and Carol Gilligan) had different experiences of privilege and different ideas about what wellness would really entail for the rest of us. There were two main ideas in their work that were hella fucking radical at the time, but make nothing but intuitive sense 50 years later. They are:

1) Human beings are hardwired to connect. We get better in healthy relationships and crave interdependence, not independence. But our general ideas about mental health are still focused generally on being independent rather than relating with others to support our wellness.

2) We are the products of all sorts of fuckedupedness. If your world is disrupted on a regular basis because of who you are, what you look like, and where you live, you lack privilege in those areas. And lacking privilege makes you far more susceptible to mental health issues and less likely to receive appropriate treatment for them.

What they were pointing out was not only had Industrialized Western culture shifted to dismiss the role of emotions in decision-making, but that we've also had huge shifts in how people perceive the importance of relationships. Further, the gaps in mechanisms of privilege between groups with privilege and groups without have gotten larger.

Emotions matter. Privilege matters. Relationships matter. And we live in a time where all these things are undervalued and dismissed. Rollo May had been the first to glimpse that historical shift when looking at how philosophical thought was changing throughout time. These disruptions have been happening at warp speed since the dawning of the Industrial Age. In the 19th century.

It's really fucking hard to tolerate uncertainty, disruption, and change in all aspects of one's life when you are disallowed from exploring your true identity and having it accepted and validated by larger society. We stay quiet. We dissemble. We disengage. Fearful isn't the right word because it's usually more insidious even than a specific, identifiable threat. When you fear something, you have the opportunity to move away from it. Exhaustion, overwhelm, a sense of non-belonging are internal experiences with no identifiable specific threat, and this lack of specific threat is why the symptoms of anxiety cover so much ground. At its coolest setting, it can be the experience of unease. At medium heat, it's distress. At a full boil, it's straight up panic. And it's a hugely somatic experience. That is, it's something you feel in your body as much as something that controls your thoughts.

And it's the most uncomfortable feeling ever. Your body is intentionally making you feel off balance so you have to attend to it. There's a fancy term for that: **disequilibrium.**

So here is our working definition: *Anxiety is a state of full body disequilibrium at a level of intensity that demands immediate attention and corrective action on your part. It can be in the face of a real or perceived threat, either present or anticipated.*

That right there is why anxiety is so hard to ignore. The whole point of the body producing that feeling is to demand your full attention like a naked, raging toddler running through the street in a snowstorm with a fist full of gummy bears in one hand and a bloody machete in the other.

Quite a visual right? Sure as hell not something you can readily disregard in the course of your day.

Anxiety demands every ounce of attention we have, no matter how inconvenient the time or unnecessary the anxiety actually was to begin with. If you have the kind of history that tells you to constantly be on guard, it's really easy for anxiety to be the default setting.

Let's look at what's going on chemically. Like I mentioned earlier, I don't ask anyone to do anything without explaining why. So this info will be important later in the book, I'm not just nerding out, pinky swear.

The Sciency Shit of the Anxiety Response

The neurocircuitry of anxiety disorders are essentially the same as the human fear circuits. Fear is an emotion designed to motivate us into defensive behaviors based on a *specific threat* we notice in the environment. The only difference between that and anxiety is that anxiety is responding to a *non-specific threat*.

There are a ton of areas of the brain associated with a fear response. The amygdala is a big one but parts of the entire brain, prefrontal regions down to specific brain stem nuclei get involved, so we are primed to respond to threats that we have familiarity with (trauma conditioning) and threats that are brand new fuckery that we have never seen before.

Short version: We are wired to have strong emotional responses because those responses keep us alive. Feeling anxious is absolutely an important survival skill.

It is one of those "seems pretty obvious, why isn't science looking at this" situations wherein the neurocircuitry of the stress response and the fear/anxiety response have extensive overlap.

(Yes, hi, no shit, right?)

The researchers who have studied how they impact each other have found that how the HPA axis works is "highly relevant" to how the brain lights up in cases of fear and anxiety . . . meaning that these responses are definitely interrelated and out there influencing each other.

The theory that makes the most sense thus far is that chronic stress leads to *anxiety sensitivity*. Anxiety sensitivity refers to how we get exhausted, burned out, and freaked out by our symptoms of stress and anxiety, which in turn makes them worse. And anxiety sensitivity is a pretty big risk factor for developing an anxiety disorder.

If you are thinking "makes sense but what's your point?" good question. Remember when I said any intervention I suggest makes sense based on our science-ing? Recognizing our relationship with our stress response and anxiety sensitivity is a really important part to managing both of them. In fact, a lot of research shows that this work (often referred to as metacognitive therapy, thought defusion techniques, and the like because we are assholes with our big and clunky words) is more efficacious than just the traditional models of cognitive behavior therapy alone.

But firstly, let's unpack all the symptoms of anxiety that are making us over-exhausted and burned out. Some of them you may have already connected to your own anxiety experience, others may surprise you. Oftentimes we feel we are being weird or quirky and not realizing that we are responding to an emotional health challenge.

What Anxiety Feels Like

So if anxiety is an emotional response that shows itself in very physical ways, what might those ways actually look like?

Thoughts and Feelings Symptoms

- Excessive worry

- Rumination (hamster wheel thinking patterns)

- Irritability/anger (Weird, right? Anger is the culturally allowed emotion so we substitute that one a lot for what we are really feeling

- Irrational fears/specific phobias

- Stage fright/social phobias

- Hyper self-awareness/self-consciousness

- Feelings of fear

- A sense of helplessness

- Flashbacks

- Obsessive behaviors, pickiness

- Compulsive behaviors

- Self doubt

- A sense that you are "losing it" or "going crazy"

Physical Body Symptoms[2]

- Trouble falling asleep or staying asleep

- Inability to rest

- Muscle tension

- Neck tension

- Chronic indigestion

- Stomach pain and/or nausea

- Racing heart

- Pulsing in the ear (feeling your heartbeat)

- Coldness, numbness or tingling in toes, feet, hands, or fingers

- Sweating

---

2 You are probably reading the physical body checklist and thinking . . . this is the same list for everything from anxiety to Ebola. Which is why so many people end up in emergency rooms thinking they are having a heart attack when they are having an anxiety attack. It's *also* the same reason many people have missed the fact that they were having a heart attack because they were also having an anxiety attack. In Mental Health First Aid training (mentalhealthfirstaid.org), we suggest that if you see someone with potential anxiety attack symptoms, you ask them if they know what is going on and has it happened before. If they say "no" then treat it like the potential emergency situation it may be and call 911.

- Weakness

- Shortness of breath

- Dizziness

- Lightheadedness

- Chest pain

- Feeling hot and cold (feeling like having chills and fever without running a temperature)

- Shooting pains/feeling like you have had an electric shock

Other "Lesser-known" Symptoms

- Perfectionism

- Indecisiveness

- Brain fog

- Depersonalization

- Avoidance

- Fatigue

- Low tolerance

Am I low-key just a more anxious person or do I have an anxiety disorder?

Clinically speaking, if you say it's a problem, I will agree that it's a problem. You know you the best.

Some people want a more formal way to self-check. There are a lot of anxiety assessment scales out there. The one you see quite often is the OASIS (which stands for Overall Anxiety Severity and Impairment Scale). It's well backed up by research and it's free to use, since it was developed by the National Institutes of Health (NIH).

OASIS doesn't have a magic cut-off number (as in: below this you are fine, above this you are batshit anxious). But it can be a good starting point for opening a conversation with a treatment provider or even just to reflect on your experiences.

The OASIS questions ask for you to reflect on your experiences over the past week and rate them on a scale of 0-4, with 0 being no probs, 1 being infrequent, 2 being occasional, 3 being pretty frequent, and 4 being constant fucking companion, thanks for the reminder.

Yeah, I'm translating a bit there. You can see the entire scale with the exact wording online, download it and print it if you want. (tinyurl.com/jnubjvx)

The exact questions are as follows:

- In the past week, how often have you felt anxious?

- In the past week, when you have felt anxious, how intense or severe was your anxiety?

- In the past week, how often did you avoid situations, places, objects, or activities because of anxiety or fear?

- In the past week, how much did your anxiety interfere with your ability to do the things you needed to do at work, at school, or at home?

- In the past week, how much has anxiety interfered with your social life and relationships?

Stress and Anxiety: Wonder Twins, Activate

Chronic stress is totally a sign of a capitalist hellscape within which there is a huge divide between those who are reasonably secure and those who are barely surviving on a razor's edge, which is most of us. And chronic stress is felt by all of us, even the reasonably secure. Fitting into the norm doesn't protect us after all.

Too much? Too political?, I'd rather that be a ridiculous and overinflated assessment but it isn't. We are working harder and longer and for less. And socioeconomic status has direct ties, at a population level, to poor mental health outcomes, which I wrote about in my book *Unfuck Your Worth*, if you're interested. But for the purpose of *this* book, I'm going to rein in my fury at corporate overlords and billionaires and focus on chronic stress and the impact of it on our mental health. And then, because I don't believe in just dumping a bunch of tragedy porn in anyone's lap, what we can actually do to combat the effects of all of this in our own lives.

UCLA researchers have been conducting simple cultural stress level check-ins by means of a poll asking people if they were "overwhelmed by all I have to do." Here's the numbers over time:

18% in 1985

29% in 2010

41% in 2017

Task load alone (not taking into account, you know . . . economic instability, institutional racism, worldwide pandemics, etc) is exhausting close to half of us at any given time. But what do these numbers actually translate to in real life?

Physiologist Walter Canon first proposed the idea of the "acute stress response" in 1915. His use of the term stress comes from the engineering field. Stress, in the context of engineering, refers to the *pressure or tension imposed upon material objects.* Because (no shit) we are also material objects and experience pressure or tension on our state of being.

But in a clinical sense, **stress** refers to *any event that requires an output of resources.*

Stress can be good (output of resources to create art, or run a race, or finish school) or it can be bad (coping with a car accident or an illness or being terminated from a job). Kelly McGoniginal, in her book *The Upside of Stress* defines stress in terms of meaning.

Things are stressful to us because they fucking matter to us.

Whether the situation is good or bad, we can hit a point where we run out of the resources that we need to cope with the situation. And that is what **distress** is. The point of resource depletion. The point where we need support. The point where you need resources. It isn't something you can do on your own. It isn't a term that identifies someone as tragically fucked up. It's a clinical term that we understand to mean this person needs some help.

And our stress numbers are through the roof, worldwide, according to the data collected within Gallup's 2018 Negative Experience Index. The index tracks the human experience of stress, anger, pain, sadness, and worry throughout the world.

In 2017, the global index score hit a new high score of 30.[3] All of the markers of negative experiences went up in 2017 except anger (yeah, I dunno why not either). And stress and worry numbers went up the most, with almost 4 out of every ten people reporting stress and worry.

So our stress levels are ridiculously high (raise your hand if you are at all surprised). And this also has a significant impact on our anxiety levels. And the science of how stress and anxiety feed each other is a really important part of better managing both of them. From the moment I could toddle and babble, I wanted to understand the reasoning behind anything I was told to do by anyone. This didn't make parenting me a pleasant experience, I imagine. But it's made me a better clinician because I want to make sure everyone else on Team Question Everything understands the reasoning behind everything I suggest as a therapist. So let's dig in and geek out.

The Science-y Shit Of The Stress Response

Before we talk about how this feels in the body, let's talk about the underlying circuitry of what's chemically going on.

The Hypothalamic-Pituitary-Adrenal (HPA) Axis is the term we use for the intertwining of the body's endocrine system and the central nervous system.

---

3 Out of 100. And each country gets its own score. For example, the score for Iraq stands at 51 as of this writing.

In a nutshell, a substance known as corticotropin-releasing factor (CRF) regulates the HPA axis. CRF is released from the hypothalamus, which binds to receptors on the pituitary gland, which releases the adrenocorticotropic hormone (ACTH), which binds to its receptors on the adrenal cortex, which then stimulates the release of hormones, primarily cortisol. More on cortisol in a sec. Now that we are all activated, the adrenal gland has special cells[4] that produce the hormone adrenaline. Adrenaline (also called epinephrine) ups our heart rate, our blood pressure, expands our ability to take more air in our lungs, makes our pupils expand so we can take in more visually, and redistributes blood to our muscles. It gets us ready for action.

And you've probably heard more about cortisol being the stress hormone, right? That's because cortisol is slower-acting in the system than adrenaline. It takes more time to build up in the body, and takes longer to dissipate back out. When we are trying to test someone's chronic stress levels, we look at cortisol. It's the best "stress average" number we have since it moves in more slowly and moves out more slowly than adrenaline. Cortisol levels going up is also correlated with vagal tone going down (as measured by heart rate variability), meaning we are far less likely to remain in our window of tolerance, to use the language of previous chapters.

---

4 Specifically? Chromaffin cells of the adrenal medulla, which are innervated by the splanchnic nerve.

It's kinda like how we can test our blood sugar at any given moment to see what it's doing, but if we want to see how well we are managing our blood sugar over the course of a few weeks or months, we get a more accurate picture from A1C lab levels. Like looking at your A1Cs as a measure of your blood sugar over time, not just your blood sugar. Or like how one grade doesn't reflect how you did across the whole semester, necessarily. You feel me on this, right?

Cortisol is a total asshole if it's something we have in our system on the regular. This whole response of the body makes evolutionary sense. It protected us from predators, right? But that's not modern life and we are not suited to having this chronic chemical cascade going all the time in the face of everyday stressors.

You've probably heard about how cortisol causes belly fat and heart attacks?

That's because it changes the body's metabolism by altering our blood glucose when it is in our system all the damn time because it's suppressing the immune system. Cortisol also increases amygdala activation and brakes hippocampal activity (which keeps the hippocampus from going in and telling the amygdala to calm its tits) . . . *Which leads to more cortisol production* (thanks, brain!).

It also makes our Prefrontal Cortex (PFC), the thinking part of the brain, far less effective. Chronic stress operates much like traumatic stress, creating "functional holes" that can be seen when SPECT imaging (Single Photon Emission Computed Tomography) is used to determine blood flow and activity in the brain. Stress diverts blood flow from the prefrontal cortex to the reactive brain and creates the interaction between the glucocorticoid receptors and dopamine that only affects stress-related dopamine production (not happy fun times dopamine production). So we have executive memory function *only* during stress related PFC dopamine flooding.

(Which is why you feel like you can't think straight when you are really stressed out . . . because you can't think straight when you are really stressed out).

It's like driving a car and you get stuck in 5th gear. You may still technically be the one driving, but the actual amount of control you have over the car is pretty low. You're kinda just looking for a pile of hay to crash into to avoid as much damage as possible, right?

What's the Diagnosis, Doc?

When we are trying to figure out if we are dealing with a lot of stress and anxiety or we have an anxiety disorder, we're looking at the impact on life domain functioning. That is (or should be) the general basis for any diagnoses. We all have emotional responses, weird thoughts, wonky behaviors, and jangly bodily reactions that we can look back on and go *"ew, not the best response there, was it?"* But when those thoughts and emotions and behaviors and somatic experiences start taking over all the time and influencing our ability to do the shit we want to do and live the life we want to live? That's when we start looking at diagnoses.

Generalized Anxiety Disorder

This diagnosis focuses on what the internetz usually terms free-floating anxiety. It's persistent and excessive all the live-long day. It's the brain saying "What if???" and us saying "What if what???" and the brain saying *"I dunno what if tho?!"* It's tension and worry and it has its physical counterpart in feeling restless, struggling to concentrate, feeling edgy (jangly nervous system), soreness from constant muscle tension, trouble sleeping, etc.

Even though it is generalized, the brain will try to attach it to something, so it may leech onto worries about work, school, responsibilities, health, relationships, chores, etc. Good times. Thanks, brain.

2 to 3 percent of the population has a generalized anxiety disorder.

Panic Disorder

Unlike our friend GAD, a panic disorder is diagnosed by . . . probably quite obviously . . . recurrent panic attacks. A panic attack is the body hitting overwhelm in terms of emotional and physical distress. Panic attack symptoms will include any number of these symptoms in some kind of clusterfuck combination designed to fuck up your life epically: Heart palpitations or rapid heart beat, sweating, shaking, trembling, tight chest, chest pain, shortness of breath, feeling like you can't catch your breath, feeling light-headed or dizzy or faint, feeling like your throat is closing up or you're choking, hot flashes, chills, stomach pain or nausea, tingling, numbness, feeling out of control, worrying you're dying, or disassociation (feeling disconnected from your body).

2 to 3 percent of the population has a panic disorder.

Specific Phobias

A specific phobia is one that is a persistent and excessive fear of a specific thing or situation that is generally not harmful. It's about an out-size response to what's in front of you or what you are thinking about. If a cottonmouth tells you to get the fuck up out of their lake, you git. But a little corn snake chilling on a rock taking a nap shouldn't provoke a huge panic response. Or a video of a snake on YouTube, or thinking about a snake (as one does) when none are around.

While someone without a phobia may go "gross, snake" if they don't really like them, people with a phobia know that their reaction is way oversized but they can't overcome it and will start to go to pretty big lengths to avoid what they fear, for example missing saying goodbye to a dying loved one because they are unable to get on a plane due to a flying phobia.

7 to 9 percent of the population has a specific phobia.

Agoraphobia

Agoraphobia is usually listed separately from the other specific phobias because it's not a fear of the literal outside, but the anxiety of being stuck in specific situations without support or means of escape if a panic attack occurs. Agoraphobia is diagnosed when two or more of the following become a problem for you:

- Using public transportation
- Being in open spaces
- Being in enclosed places
- Standing in line or being in a crowd
- Being outside the home alone

. . . and the fear has been present 6 months or longer. The time part is super important because a traumatic event can make you wary for some time about certain situations but you will eventually recalibrate and be able to go places again.

Agoraphobia is an outsized response that gets worse over time instead of better.

2 percent of the population has agoraphobia.

Social Anxiety Disorder (Also Known as Social Phobia)

A person with social anxiety disorder experiences significant worry that they are being watched and judged by others, and rejection, embarrassment, and humiliation will result. Individuals with social anxiety will often go to great lengths to avoid social situations or endure them with constant anxiety leading to exhaustion. Like the other anxiety disorders, the symptoms have to be present for 6 months or more and it has to be impacting daily functioning.

7 percent of the population has social anxiety disorder.

Separation Anxiety Disorder

We think of separation anxiety as something only small children suffer from. Although most of the people with a separation anxiety disorder are young, adults can struggle with it as well. Separation anxiety happens when we become excessively anxious and fearful about being away from someone to whom we are attached, to the point that it is causing life domain issues. The fears may include losing the person in question or not being able to care for themselves without that person. Separation anxiety is diagnosed in children when it has occurred four weeks or longer, for adults it is 6 months or longer.

1 to 2 percent of the population have a separation anxiety disorder.

Wait . . . . Isn't OCD an Anxiety Disorder?

Before the DSM-5, there were other common diagnoses that were listed as anxiety disorders that still exist but are now in different categories. PTSD and acute stress (which is essentially an earlier, shorter-term trauma response) are the ones that made obvious sense to everyone since trauma responses are nervous system injuries, not anxiety disorders (despite adding the word stress to the name).

The one that most befuddled people was the removal of Obsessive-Compulsive Disorder from the list of anxiety disorders, I think it's really helpful to explain why it's now considered an entirely different phenotype.

First of all, OCD almost always co-occurs with anxiety. But the OCD is *creating* anxiety, which is why treating the OCD first will typically extinguish much of the anxiety response. As we geeked out about earlier, anxiety is an emotion processing issue caused by an over-activation of the fear response, but the neurochemistry of OCD is entirely different.

OCD involves problems with activation of the prefrontal striatal cortex caudate nucleus, the thymus, and the orbital gyri which are all tied to executive functioning. Additionally, people with OCD typically have other executive functioning issues including struggles with cognitive flexibility and the capacity to shift between tasks. OCD is essentially a form of *neurodivergence*.

The cycle that an OCD brain gets trapped in involves either obsessions, compulsions, or both.

Obsessions are thoughts, ideas, or images that are unwanted and won't go away. They tend to be really dark and distressing and fucked up. Exposure to germs that make them or others terribly sick is often a big one, as are images of causing horrible harm to someone or something (like accidentally killing someone or burning down a house). Sexual and religious images, because we have such strong cultural messages about what is appropriate or not, are also a common topic of obsessive thoughts. Compulsions are behaviors that you feel you have to carry out over and over again to relieve your anxiety. If you have OCD, it is common to have compulsions, mental acts or rituals around cleaning, counting, checking, requesting or demanding reassurance, and ensuring order and symmetry.

The compulsive behaviors are our brains adaptations to the obsessive thoughts that the brain comes up with to help manage how horrible and shitty those thoughts are. The thoughts themselves are the brain's way of trying to prevent something awful from happening. They provide relief for a little bit, but then have to be performed again and again like whack-a-mole. Sometimes they have a direct connection, like washing obsessively because of the obsession with germs, and sometimes they aren't realistically related, but provide the brain with an idea that it has a little more control, like creating rules and rituals as protection, like a superstition on steroids such as "if I only wear blue clothes no one in my family will die."

So while OCD produces anxiety, it is far more complex than anxiety and is treated somewhat differently.

Medical Issues That Can Be Mistaken For Anxiety Disorders

Anxiety is intentionally producing a *"holy shit we're all about to die"* response that is like 99.44% physical, right? It is barely possible to live with that level of fear on a daily basis. Because anxiety is so physical, many diseases that *are* purely physical get dismissed as anxiety. Because real medical issues get dismissed so often (especially among women, all people of color, etc.) keeping in mind that there may be other things that should be ruled out is really important.

A useful mnemonic device, "THINC MED," developed by a Georgetown University psychiatrist and functional medicine specialist named Robert Hedaya, helps docs (and anyone needing to advocate for further testing) remember what might be some other causes for anxiety symptoms.

T (Tumors): Because anxiety is activated by fear circuitry in the brain, brain tumor placement may activate that circuit. Brain tumors cause a wide range of psychological symptoms, including anxiety, personality changes and hallucinations, along with physically creating excess adrenaline in the body. If the anxiety is accompanied by headaches, high blood pressure, and the like, ruling out a possible tumor may make sense.

H (Hormones): Several hormonal issues can look like anxiety. Thyroid and parathyroid problems are the most common, and adrenal gland problems are also high on the list. If you also are experiencing restlessness, sleep issues, tremors, weight changes, and heat intolerance, consider having your hormones checked. And for individuals that menstruate? Estrogen can also prompt anxiety during menstrual cycle fluctuations and during menopause, so tracking your cycle along with anxiety symptoms may give you some insight.[5]

I (Infectious Diseases): There are multiple infectious diseases that can produce symptoms that look like anxiety such as Lyme disease from tick bites and untreated strep infections. Other diseases that are more rare include Guillain-Barre syndrome which is neurological and occurs after a viral infection. Along with anxiety, it causes progressive weakness and difficulty breathing.

N (Nutrition): Deficiencies, overload, and malabsorption issues can mimic emotional disorders. In my book *Unfuck Your Body*, I talk about how common deficiencies of certain nutrients can be (up to 70% of individuals have a magnesium deficiency for example). Many deficiencies will have anxiety as the first symptom that your body is struggling (B-12 for example). Issues with gut absorption or having had gastric bypass surgery increase the risk of these

---

5 This isn't true for anyone who is taking estrogen for gender confirmation or menopausal symptoms for any other medical reasons. All of the studies of medically necessary estrogen treatments show a *decrease* in anxiety in the individuals taking it, presumably because the amount in the system is stable, not in flux as with menstrual cycles.

issues as well, and you may need supplementation support even if you are a healthy eater.

C (Central nervous system): Traumatic brain injury (acquired head trauma which includes concussions), even pretty mild cases can injure the nervous system, making anxiety far more likely. Other neurological conditions, especially ones that are chronic and progressive are strongly correlated with anxiety, such as dementia, myasthenia gravis, and Guillain-Barre.

M (Miscellaneous): Miscellaneous here means any miscellaneous diseases and pain conditions. There are a lot of rare diseases like porphyria (a blood metabolism disorder) and Wilson's disease (a genetic problem with metabolizing copper) that are associated with anxiety disorders. As are food allergies, rheumatoid disorders, inflammatory conditions, chronic headaches, IBS, sleep disorders, and fibromyalgia.

E (Electrolyte abnormalities and environmental toxins): Anything that disturbs your electrolytes, which can include disordered dieting and even many medical therapies, can lead to anxiety. Environmental toxins are another nervous system disruptor that can be at play. Organophosphate insecticides have been linked to anxiety disorders, and more and more research is showing that a good amount of the population is electromagnetically sensitive and anxiety is a common symptom.

D (Drugs): And yes this includes the use of recreational drugs, illicit or not, as well as the ones we take for reasons other than enjoyment. Many prescription drugs and over the counter drugs can increase anxiety. And yes, this can include herbal supplements. Good old caffeine is still on the naughty list, and food additives (MSG has been the most studied) have also been linked to anxiety disorders. Detoxing any drugs or medications can cause anxiety as part of the withdrawal symptoms, as well.

I know, this list is like . . . so, *everything*? I don't include all this information to give you a sense of overwhelm, but instead to give you a sense of hope. A lot of very real physical issues cause the body to react with upregulated fear circuitry. If you are doing everything to manage your anxiety and it is still the biggest motherfucker in your life, there might be a physical cause or a physical amplifier that hasn't been addressed.

I always suggest tracking your anxiety not just over the years (like my senior year sucked ass but the rest of high school was fine) but when it's worse over the course of a day, week, or month. And looking at your lab work, and your toxin exposures, and all that other information that might be playing a role. Be willing to experiment. A lot of things may seem odd but are free to try, such as turning off your wireless at night and putting your phone in airplane mode and seeing if you sleep better without as much "dirty electricity" in your space. I have had some major wins as a clinical nutritionist helping clients better manage their anxiety by looking at what is going on in their bodies, not just in their heads.

Anxiety and Its Favorite Cousins

Adding anxiety to depression is a bit like adding cocaine to alcohol. It presses fast-forward on the whole experience."

—Matt Haig, *Reasons To Stay Alive*

While anxiety can come along for the ride with any mental health issue, some are more common than others. Mood disorders are the big one: anxiety occurs very often with chronic stress, dysthymia, depression, and bipolar disorder. Anxiety is an over-response to stimuli and depressive symptoms can be the opposite side of that coin, as a response to the exhaustion of hypervigilance.

Anxiety is also very common with autism spectrum disorders (anxiety disorders are the most common co-occurring disorders among people with autism), ADHD (especially adult ADHD), eating disorders, and body dysmorphic disorder.

If you resonate with the symptoms and experiences of anxiety it may not be "just a part of your [insert other diagnosis]." Discuss including specific treatment for anxiety with your treatment team. You can always look at whether or not the anxiety is still present once the other issues are stable . . . but it's pretty hard to stabilize other issues when your fear circuits are on fire all the time.

Who Gets An Anxiety Disorder

Soooo many of us, y'all.

Anxiety disorders are the most common psychiatric diagnosis in the US. Almost 30% of the population will experience a "diagnosable illness" level of anxiety at some point in their lives. And in any given year, 18% of adults ages 18 and older meet the criteria for an anxiety disorder.

And this diagnosis often results in significant debilitation and can lead to other chronic medical problems that affect multiple organs and body systems. The associated healthcare costs associated with anxiety disorders is greater than $40 billion each year.

(Never mind the bump in numbers from worldwide pandemics and the ensuing chaos. The numbers we are seeing currently will be bumping that "lifetime prevalence" number up in the next couple of years.)

Ok, first the genetic component. As mentioned above, anxiety isn't in and of itself a bad thing to be avoided at all costs. Elsewhere in the animal kingdom, having members of the group that are on higher alert than the others tends to be life saving. And this is no different than in humans. 30-40% of the cases of clinical anxiety demonstrate a genetic or epigenetic component. Meaning, we inherited it just like our eye color. This inheritable component also has something to do with the fact that cis women are twice as likely than cis men to have anxiety disorders. Research shows that it's far harder for us to extinguish our fear responses, again pointing to some evolutionary advantage to being on guard.

The other factors that come into play include age, sexual orientation, gender, socioeconomic status, and marital status. People who are divorced or separated, are unemployed, are the stay-at-home partner, or generally financially stressed are at higher risk. Younger people are more likely to have an anxiety disorder, in fact 75% of individuals with an anxiety disorder had their first episode before age 21.

While there are virtually no population-based health studies of adults which have explored associations between sexual attraction and health outcomes, and none at all that look at all the facets of sexuality, generally speaking gay, lesbian, and polysexual individuals have rates of anxiety that are 1.5% to 2.5% above the national average.

Among asexual individuals, both men and women are more likely to report an anxiety disorder, and the difference was much higher for ace men than ace women. Transgender and nonbinary individuals are six times more likely to have an anxiety disorder. (There is no published data seperating different non-cis identities at the time of publication—nonbinary folks are generally lumped in with binary trans individuals, if mentioned at all.)

Individuals with intersex conditions also report higher instances of anxiety (again 2 times the national average), though none of the studies parsed out differences among birth assigned sex, gender identity, sexual orientation, and other possible contributing factors . . . or even the type of intersex condition they were born with.

When we look at anxiety disorders co-occuring with physical illness, the numbers get even wonkier. Some studies show that people start with an anxiety disorder, which leads to a poorer quality of life and an increase in likelihood of getting more medical problems. Other studies demonstrate that people get sick and then develop both anxiety and depression in far greater numbers. There isn't any solid data to identify which is the chicken and which is the egg . . . or even if the combination is organic, reactive, or some kind of wibbly-wobbly combination (though that is most likely). And other factors come into play around the nature of the illness, the duration of the illness, our age when all the shit hits the fan, etc. etc. We know it happens but there isn't a lot of solid hows and whys.

So we don't have great data. Shocking, I know.

But we do have enough to show that these higher rates are often related to what researchers term "minority stress" meaning lack of societal power and privilege. And it isn't an inherent part of someone's personhood. When the related stressors are mitigated, the anxiety rates drop as well. For example, among individuals who are transgender, having social identity affirmation and access to gender affirming lowers those rates of anxiety back down to that of the general average.

So we have the genetics component, just like we have a genetics component to most every mental health diagnosis. But we also have a huge number of individuals whose anxiety is related to the external factors and circumstances of the world around them. And then there's those of us who have the fuckery of dealing with both. How we even express our anxiety brings us back to our individual cultural contexts, and how we can best *manage* our anxiety brings us back to our personal anxiety etiology. Genetics? Societal disconnect? Both?

I talk to people regularly who have "failed" at anxiety management because these things were not taken into account as part of their treatment planning. So everything else we talk about in this book will reference back to this information, in order to help you better advocate for your care.

Does Anxiety Look Different to Different People?

One thing you likely noticed in the preceding section was no info on ethnicity and anxiety disorders. I could have mentioned it and said "yeah, those numbers are weird so we don't really know" but when it comes to ethnicity and culture it goes a bit deeper.

Here's the weird: Racial discrimination is associated with the endorsement of various anxiety disorders over and over (and over and over) in the research, yet even when controlling for other demographic variables like age, gender, and socioeconomic status White Americans continue to report symptoms of anxiety disorders (and depressive disorders for that matter) far more than any ethnic minority group.

Researchers have suggested a lot of different reasons for this discrepancy including differential recall/differential experience of the symptoms (it is not noted as depression or anxiety by the person experiencing it or they don't remember it as anxiety because it was just *life*), selective non-response (the person in the study is choosing to not share their experience with researchers), measurement bias (the questions being asked to ascertain anxiety suck at measuring what anxiety looks like in people of color).

The answer is quite likely all of the above. I know that as a therapist and as a bi-racial parent. My son had horrible, overwhelming anxiety that he expressed through anger. Anger gave him a sense of control over that which made him fearful. My oldest was simply avoidant of things that were anxiety-provoking, in that way that femme-presenting children can get away with because it is dismissed as shyness. It took significant work to uncover the real issue and help them learn to express and work with the underlying anxiety, reducing the need for them to use the other coping behaviors they had developed over the years.

Additionally, our cultural norms and belief systems will also shift how we articulate anxiety. This is referred to as differences in ethnophysiology and ethnopsychology.

For an ethnophysiology example, someone who is from the United States may fear tightness in the chest as a *heart attack*, where someone from Cambodia may fear a *wind attack* because where we may use the word veins, a Cambodian individual may use the word tubes (sâsai). In reality, both people are referring to the same thing, *a blockage that can cause death,* though the different terminology means that one person's concern may be dismissed as primitive, superstitious, and silly. The underlying physiology is exactly the same, one isn't more superstitious or sillier than the other. But the *communication* of that physiology may not jibe with that of a treatment provider.

For an ethnopsychology example, Japanese and Korean cultures have a specific form of social anxiety called aijin kyofusho (TKS) which refers to doing something in public that embarrasses or offends the people around them. This exists elsewhere in the world of course, but it isn't a cultural norm here in South Texas to worry about *someone else* being embarrassed by our behavior. The stricter the social rules and the social norms, the higher the levels of anxiety for people.

I continue to be astonished by the number of licensed clinicians who have never heard of the *cultural formulation interview* in their DSM-V[6] which is actually quite useful. So soapbox speech for my people who work in the field. Whether using the CFI or something else, please take into account the possibility that someone is presenting an issue in a way that doesn't match a traditional diagnostic. We need to look more deeply at how people describe, experience, and interpret their experiences. Training and consultation can help, as can even a little research before diagnosing.

And if you are reading this for yourself, if something jiggles loose regarding how your family interpreted your experiences, that is absolutely something to bring up with whomever you are receiving treatment from. Maybe if you were always *que nervious* about school your whole childhood, that might be an important signifier that you have always struggled with a level of social anxiety. You may not check off the "right" boxes at first glance, but that doesn't mean you aren't experiencing a very real mental health issue.

---

6 This is an evidence-based series of questions designed to help clinicians make person-centered cultural assessments to incorporate into their diagnosis and treatment planning. The number of clinicians who do not know this exists continues to make my left eye twitch.

UNFUCK YOUR
ANXIETY

The brilliant thing about anxiety is it allows us the opportunity to anticipate and plan how to manage life.

The complete fuckitude of anxiety is it allows us the opportunity to anticipate and plan out how to manage life *in all the fucking horrible ways it can go wrong at all times and ugh just fuck it all in the ear I'm going back to bed.*

So how? How do you do any of it? How do you do this life-ing thing when your PJs are far more comfortable than any other clothing you own and it's all such bullshit, anyway?

Mostly, because you want to, at least at some level. And it's worth it, at most levels.

Here's what you do:

1) **Self care.** Self-care isn't a one and done thing, it has to be a central part of our lives. It can mean a nice mug of tea but

it can also mean going to the dentist and making a budget. It's ongoing, it's not always the fun stuff, and you have to keep doing it. Like all the fucking time. Getting better doesn't mean stop doing the things that got you better, right? It's like tossing the antibiotics before you finished the whole course of treatment. Except the whole course of treatment may be taking care of yourself gently for the rest of your life. And you're allowed to. And supposed to. Keep up with that.

2) **Talk about it**. Talking about it doesn't mean emotionally vomiting all over everyone. It means explaining your reactions. Something like "Do you read Jenny Lawson? I'm totally having a Blogess anxiety moment right now. I'm not trying to be an asshole, but today has been fucked for me. I'm gonna go grab some water and be back in a second." Boom, it's that easy. It's amazing how supportive people can actually be if you give them the chance. If you try to talk to someone and they are dismissive and unempathic, then they are either total assholes (and fuck them) or they are dealing with their own shit and don't know how to be there for you (so fuck them, at least for now).

3) **Ask for help.** Because, seriously. It takes far more courage and strength to ask for and receive help than it does to give help. Give people a chance to help you, but give them that information in very specific ways like "Can you come sit

with me at my doctor's appointment/come with me to walk my dogs/meet with me for coffee and discuss the complete mindfuck the OA was for me?" And if they say no, then we are back to saying, fuck them. You were brave to ask. Keep asking. And think of it like any other ATM. But with help instead of cash. You put in help when you have it to give, and you take out help when you need it.

4) **Create**. That Rollo May dude I was talking about? He cited interesting research that shows that the best way to manage anxiety is to first be able to sit with it. Which makes sense. If you can't even tolerate it, you certainly won't be able to find ways to manage it. And the research shows that creative people are the best at finding ways to sit with it. So get creative. Write it out. Make art. Putting things out there in the world helps us be more authentically who we are. Anxiety and all.

5) **Know your rights**. If you are in work or school and your anxiety is super batshit, you do have legal protections if you need accommodations and if your employer has 15 employees or more. Federal law requires you to try to figure out how to resolve any problem and request a reasonable accommodation. You will likely have to provide documentation of your anxiety diagnosis. But you can't be fired for outing your anxiety and asking for your desk to be moved to a quieter location, or

something else entirely reasonable. You can see more about ADA rules here: eeoc.gov/facts/fs-ada.html

Learning Your Triggers

Sometimes we know straight up what our triggers are gonna be.

We know a first date or a public speaking engagement or a meeting with our boss is going to send our anxiety through the roof. We know a road trip where we can't find a clean rest stop with a non-sketch bathroom is gonna cause a freak out (And why is there *not* an app for that??? The struggle is *real*).

But sometimes? Not a fucking clue. Like all other mental health issues, we may have a genetic predisposition to anxiety and/or it may be a product of the environment we grew up in or live in now. And that can make figuring out our specific triggers difficult.

A mood tracking diary (either an app or old school paper one) feels like a lot of work, but can really help with figuring out your triggers. You can use the super-simple template on the facing page. If you need help figuring out the exact right word to describe what's going on in your body, do an Internet image search for "feelings word wheel."

Any of the exercises in the next section can be used to help manage anxiety in the moment. Give your anxiety a goofy name or persona. Carry ice to hold as a reminder. Do some deep breathing exercises.

And then, when you aren't feeling anxious, you can work on longer-term self-training to rewire your brain.

We are including a fancy mood tracker in the accompanying workbook but you can make your own. Flip a piece of paper sideways and mark off room for the following columns:

• Day of the Week

• Mood

• Situation

• Magnitude (0-100)

• Symptoms

Disrupting the Signal: Short-Term Anxiety Management

Even once you've figured out your triggers, anxiety isn't something you can willpower your way out of.

As you saw, we have the asshole twin chemical combo going on. So in the here-and-now moment of anxiety or a straight up panic attack, you gotta do something to metabolize out those chemicals. When anxiety hits, you have to fight it head on.

Here is some stuff to try:

1) **Deep Breathing and Progressive Relaxation.** Yeah, yeah. That shit is hard to fucking do when you are spun up. But it's important to at least try. Because the chemicals released during an anxiety or panic attack are designed to get your breathing ramped up and your heart racing. So it's going to add to the sense that you are going to have a heart attack or that you will stop breathing. Of course, that isn't going to happen. Try reminding your brain and body about that. Making a conscious effort to breathe and un-tense will slow the heart rate back down and help you get more oxygen flowing. It's a literal chemical counterbalance. Want detailed instructions for this? They're in a later chapter.

2) **Name That Bastard.** Give your anxiety an actual persona to inhabit. Name it after a heinous ex, a shitty grade school teacher, or Kim Jong-un. Create a whole character for your anxiety. Anxiety feels so nebulous that giving yourself someone to battle really helps. Then you can have convos with Donald Trump's Epic Hair Swirl (or whomever, but personally I think all panic attacks should be named after that hair) whenever it comes calling. You can focus on that entity the way you would an actual person that was threatening you

in a real-world situation. You can negotiate, you can yell back, you can lock it in a box. Whatever works.

3) **Create Coping Cards.** Coping statements are pretty much as simple as they sound: Mantras or reminders that help you manage your anxiety and stay in control of your body. They can be literal self-talk ("This will only last a minute") or a reminder to take a deep breath. You know, whatever helps. But the problem with coping statements is you sure as fuck aren't going to remember them in the heat of the moment. When you find mantras, facts about anxiety, or other statements or images that help you, put them on an index card. Hole punch those and put them on a snap-shut key ring and you have a set of coping cards you can flip through when panic hits. It sounds epically nerdy, I know. But I have had so many clients end up loving the shit out of their cards and using them all the time.

4) **Ride The Wave.** Avoidance is what makes it worse. Try setting aside 5 minutes to sit with the anxiety you're feeling instead of fighting back. It won't last forever, I swear on my Roomba it won't. If you attend to what you are feeling, you get over it way more quickly than if you avoid it. I've noticed I'm bored with myself about 3 minutes into committing to sitting with my feeling for 5. I'm ready to go make a cup of coffee,

read a book, find the cookies I hid from myself, or do anything other than perseverate.

5) **Put it On Ice.** We used to encourage clients to wear a rubber band and snap it on their wrist if they felt an urge to self-harm, or were having spinning thoughts, or considering an impulsive behavior. But, um, snap a rubber band on yourself enough times and you will tear the fuck up out of your skin. So we're not doing that anymore.

But the point of the rubber band was legit. We were trying to help people disrupt the current focus of the brain by encouraging it to attend to another pain point. Ice works much better without causing lasting damage. Seriously, try it. Grab an ice cube and squeeze. Your brain is gonna be all "OW! WTF you doing that for??" and it disrupts the signal. If you have an impulse to self-injure to manage anxiety, you can actually place the ice on the part of the body you typically hurt instead of doing the other harm behavior.

The cool thing too, is carrying ice with you isn't obvious. You can bop around in your day, and grab an ice cube out of your cup without people going "What the hell is that about?" I have worked in group programs where everyone carried water, so handing someone a water cup full of ice to use if they got triggered didn't make them feel singled out to their peers.

Lifestyle-Focused Treatment Strategies and Interventions

So I wrote a whole book about the mind-body connection and some of the things we can do that really help with a variety of mental illness issues. There is gonna be a lot of crossover here, since certain nutritional deficiencies and physical stressors (e.g., issues with inflammation and gut microbiota) are common with a multitude of mental and physical health issues. But this isn't a cut and paste job, pinky swear. All of the recommendations I have here have been studied specifically with anxiety disorders so nothing I suggest is guesstimatory crap.

This isn't to say that lifestyle changes will always be "enough" to treat an anxiety disorder. Therapy and/or medication may be a really important part of your treatment regimens, at least during certain periods of your life. But being as healthy as you can be will help other treatments work far more effectively. Think of lifestyle focused treatment strategies as foundational support.

Diet

An article in the American Journal of Psychiatry recently called out the profession of its readers by pointing out that anxiety is a *highly prevalent chronic illness* that is absolutely in part modulated by biological processes such as brain function and plasticity, the stress response system, inflammation, and oxidative processes. And yet the profession as a whole does not include dietary modification as part of their primary prevention and treatment strategies. The research is there, but the cohesive strategy is not. Broccoli doesn't get government subsidies and doesn't help sell medication, so it doesn't have advocacy from captains of industry. Which means it's up to us to change things from the ground up.

There are certain nutrients that we are statistically more likely to be lacking, and all of them have been associated with anxiety disorders. For example, researchers found in one study of individuals who presented at the ER with a severe panic attack had low levels of B vitamins (B6 specifically) and low iron. researchers observed the levels of B6 and iron in patients who visited the emergency room due to severe panic attack or panic induced hyperventilation. Other studies have found that zinc, magnesium, and omega-t fatty acids have all also been linked to lowered anxiety.

Additionally, probiotic rich foods, fermented foods, and foods high in antioxidants have been found to reduce anxiety, which makes sense since all of these foods promote gut healing and a reduction in chronic inflammation.

You may be thinking "okay, fine then . . . tell me what to eat for B vitamins?" It has to be something you enjoy for it to be sustainable. You may not (or cannot) eat eggs, but do like whole grains and incorporate more of those into your diet. I always recommend to people to check out resources online like the world's healthiest foods website (WHfoods.org) to match up the nutrients you need with the foods you like.

And honestly? While we may be lacking certain nutrients and paying attention to that is really important, we can't treat food like pills. Food is complex and the nutrients in food interact with each other and within our bodies. The higher the sugar content of a piece of fruit, the higher the amount of dietary fiber, typically. Therefore an apple and half a can of soda will have radically different effects on the human body.

Which means the more real food you eat in general, the better for managing your health. One of the best things you can do for the entirety of your body-mind is reduce the amount of ultra-processed foods in your diet. I'd love for you to get rid of them all together but that is pretty difficult to achieve without investing a lot of time, money, or both . . . which are things in short supply for most people. But research shows that just decreasing the amount of ultra-processed foods in our diet by 30% makes a *huge* difference in our overall health.

And while these refined sugars and chemical ingredients aren't good for anyone's body, they are especially problematic for anyone with a diagnosis. A "normie" can tolerate a

Frappuccino, a Snickers bar, or fast-food chain orange chicken and white rice with far less nervous system upset than the rest of us. If you hurt your back you don't pick up heavy things right? Same for how we nourish our bodies for other forms of recovery.

And speaking of Frappuccinos? Caffeine and anxiety is no bueno for very real, chemical reasons. The adenosine receptor system (part of the RNA building blocks that support life) mediates the buzzy effects of caffeine *and* regulates our anxiety response. Researchers have been able to narrow down the aspects of genetics that make us more likely to be anxious and respond poorly to caffeine (976T/T and the 2592Tins/ Tins genotypes if you're curious). You don't have to get your DNA sequenced or anything, just detox the caffeine and see how your anxiety is affected over the ensuing weeks.

Supplements

Okay, you're with me. Your blood work shows a ton of markers for inflammation and you are dumping out sugar and inhaling avocados like you have your own tree out back. But you are still having a hard time getting your system back online. One of the (many) problems of consistently elevated cortisol is that the body really struggles to absorb these same key nutrients *and* it down-regulates digestion which makes our gut issues chronic. This makes sense, right? Part of getting ready to fight or run means stopping digestion so that energy goes to other areas of our body. Supplementation, especially high quality whole-food supplementation (instead of synthetic vitamins) and herbal support can also really help you feed the body what it needs to get back on-line.

Whole food supplements are literally just food. You're piling on the nutrition you need for healing. In a time period where we are all missing things from our diet that our ancestors got (e.g. depleted soil means we may not be getting enough trace minerals in our diet from the veggies we eat, even if they are local and organically raised), adding those things back in can be incredibly helpful for our bodies. My motto is you have to either eat it or take it. And honestly, getting enough of the nutrients I need through diet alone is nearly impossible. Whole food supplements can help bridge that gap without the side effects of the synthetic isolates found in allopathic meds and even most over-the-counter vitamins. All of the nutrients that support anxiety management apply here including magnesium, zinc, B vitamins, D vitamins, omega-3s (either through a fish oil, a blue-green algae, or ahi flower). There are also whole food proprietary blends that can be hugely useful (the one my son used for several years was Standard Process' Minchex).

Herbal supplements work far more like medications do but also more like whole food supplements than you would first guess. Instead of treating a symptom, they are also operating to promote the body's own healing and ability to balance itself. That's why so many of the herbal remedies that are most effective for mood disorders are adaptogenic ones. This means instead of an upper or downer, they function as all-arounders. They're like the thermostat on the wall that is going to kick in heat when it's cold or the a/c when it's hot as balls. Meaning they work by promoting the stabilization of physiological processes.

Yeah, you might say, but . . . aren't supplements complete bullshit? I've read the articles.

Part of the reason that dietary supplements get a bad rap is because many of the ones on the market are complete crap. The New York Attorney General tested and sent a multitude of cease and desist letters to herbal supplement companies based on the fact that much of what they tested had no active ingredient.

And also? University of Guelph in Canada studied a bunch of supplements and found many unlisted ingredients within them, including things that could encourage an allergic response in someone taking them. Further, synthetic versions of the product, rather than the actual extracted herb or whole food, are generally going to have more side effects because the human body struggles to recognize them for what they are.

So we read about the amazingness of using something like St. John's wort, then we feel stupid and/or ripped off when it doesn't work for us. I had that experience with a cheap kava I tried years ago. It made me seriously irritable and more than a little batshit. I was afraid to try kava again until I learned more about finding and using quality products. I was great about educating myself on prescription meds, but it somehow never occurred to me that I should treat supplements just as seriously. So, takeaway? If you are using supplements (either herbal or whole food), work with a provider who knows their shit (an herbalist, Chinese medicine practitioner, clinical nutrition professional, etc.) and research anything you choose to take and the quality of the brand you are using, just like you would any other treatment.

This is a basic list of adaptogenic herbs (herbs that help promote balance in the body, rather than force a particular upper or downer response) and nervines (herbs that have a calming effect specifically on the nervous system). This is not a be-all, end-all list. For example, I'm not trained in Chinese medicine, so if your practitioner is, you may see completely different combinations or names beyond my more limited knowledge in that area.

Adaptogens For Depression: Ashwagandha, Asian ginseng, holy basil, rhaponticum, rhodiola, and schisandra.

Adaptogens for Central Nervous System Support: Asian ginseng, rhaponticum, schisandra, shilajit, ashwagandha, cordyceps, and jiaogulan.

Adaptogens for Anxiety: Ashwagandha, jiaogulan, reishi, and schisandra.

Nervine Tonic Herbs (non-adaptogenic): Blue vervain, chamomile, fresh milky oat, hawthorn, linden, motherwort, passionflower, skullcap, lemon balm, St. John's wort, mimosa, lavender, and rosemary.

Other Supportive Supplements: Tryptophan (helps depression and sleeplessness), B12 (helps increase energy), GABA (helps manage anxiety), and trace minerals (helps manage irritability).

Movement

I tend to shy away from the word exercise because it has such strong punitive associations for so many people. But when we move our bodies in ways we enjoy . . . when we *play* we actually enjoy the time we spend doing so, not just the resulting health benefits.

But, okay . . . movement. How does it affect anxiety *directly?* First of all, it changes our attention control. One of the best forms of talk therapy for anxiety is metacognitive therapy, where instead of focusing on challenging our anxious thoughts, we learn to shift focus away from them (changing how we think instead of what we think). Movement, exercise, play, whatever you call it requires an engagement of attention control which takes a large enough chunk of our working memory that our anxiety rumination automatically decreases. Additionally, this same executive function activation inhibits the mid-brain anxiety response (specifically, the PFC dials down the ventral hippocampus). And the magical endocannabinoid that everyone is talking about now and using THC, CBD, and hemp to activate? Exercise activates eCB (N-arachidonoylethanolamine [AEA] and 2-arachidonoylglycerol) for freeeeeee.

And this effect builds up over time, while we get immediate short term relief from anxiety, incorporating movement in our daily lives increases our *effortful control* over our anxiety symptoms to such a high level that one researcher called it "the virtuous circle." What kind of movement? Again, whatever you like. I wrote in *Unfuck Your Body* about the power of mindful movement for somatic awareness (like yoga and tai chi and stuff). That kind of movement is helpful specifically for anxiety, but so is high intensity training. So do whatever you can maintain motivation to continue to do!

Medical Model Interventions

I need to preface this by saying the lines between lifestyle interventions, traditional medical model interventions, and other complementary treatments have gotten really blurry. And I mean that in the best possible way. The medical establishment is more and more embracing supplements, yoga, weighted blankets, and the like as we gain more and more research on their efficacy. Something can be woo-woo as fuck and still work like a charm. So what goes in what category wasn't an easy decision. If the VA is providing reiki and acupuncture does that make it a medical model? Some people would say hell no and some people (and I fall in this category) would say absolutely yes.

But for the sake of organizational clarity, we are meaning "medical model" to mean the traditional treatments that have been around for some decades as evidence based practice. And the ones listed as complementary practices are the newer, hipper evidence based practices that maybe don't have as much evidence behind them yet but are becoming more and more integrated into the mainstream. It also means if you aren't a huge fan of the woo-woo you know which section to skip, yeah?

Talk Therapy

Obviously, I am pro talk therapy since this is my job and I still have student loans to pay off. But I can better argue my case by stating that there has been significant research on the efficacy of talk therapy for managing anxiety . . . most people do not get relief from medication alone. The most common forms of talk therapy for anxiety are Cognitive Behavior Therapy and Exposure Therapy, which is a form of behavioral therapy. Cognitive Therapy aims to modify maladaptive cognitions, self-statements or beliefs. The behavioral portion focuses on behavioral interventions that aim to decrease maladaptive behaviors and increase adaptive ones by practicing new behaviors that result in new learning.

Exposure Therapy is a strict behavioral approach, working to increase adaptive ones by modifying their antecedents and consequences and by behavioral practices that result in new learning. Exposure Therapy focuses on the behavioral portion, only focusing on exposing oneself to anxiety-producing events until the brain learns that they aren't actually fearful, which makes it particularly effective for social anxiety and phobias. As mentioned earlier in this book, extinguishing anxiety behaviors isn't a perfect science, and may be especially difficult for women due to some evolutionary differences, but it can absolutely provide some significant relief.

Other commonly used approaches have similarities to these approaches. Dialectical Behavioral Therapy (DBT) and Acceptance and Commitment Therapy (ACT) both incorporate techniques regarding mindfulness, emotional regulation, and emotional acceptance. Anxiety specific programs like MAP (Mastering and Anxiety and Panic) are also cognitive-behavioral programs that have been geared specifically to anxiety work.

A couple of "newer" approaches to treating anxiety that are proving to be effective is metacognitive therapy and somatic approaches. Metacognitive Therapy focuses more on the *how* we are thinking rather than the *what* and is especially helpful for anxiety disorders. Meaning, we get wrapped up in our beliefs about our thoughts of anxiety which makes them far worse. Rather than unpacking the anxious thought itself, the work centers on our thoughts about our thoughts including the worry, rumination, threat monitoring, thought control strategies, avoidance, and reassurance seeking that make things worse.

Somatic therapy, which has been a practice for several decades especially for trauma work, is being used more and more with other presenting issues. There is good reason for this. Somatic Therapy really began in its modern, Western incarnation through the work of Eugene Gendlin. Dr. Gendlin was working with couples and couldn't readily identify why some people were successful in their therapy goals and others were not. It wasn't correlated with the problems they presented with in therapy or anything obvious. In reviewing hundreds of hours of video footage, he recognized that the people who were most in touch with their own bodily responses and sensations in sessions were the ones that were the most successful in creating change in their lives.

He came up with a way of teaching that skill, which he called *focusing*, and coined the term the *felt sense*. The felt sense is the inner datum of how this whole situation is affecting us as a whole and *that* is an experience that moves us beyond emotions, language, and culture. Learning to be in touch with our bodies at a deeper level empowers us to not be overcome and reactionary to all the things going on that activate anxiety for us. I don't know if anxiety is something from which we *get* *better,* but I absolutely know we can *get better at it.*

So . . . which is right for you? Any of these interventions or a different one entirely? Or a mix? I pull from all of the above plus other interventions, including hypnotherapy, when working with anxiety disorders. It depends on the person, and research also backs that fact up. If you and the therapist you choose both feel that a particular intervention will be helpful, it will be. The relationship is the most important factor in healing. (And my clinician buddies? Check out Bruce Wampold's meta analytic research on the topic!) The interventions are the tools you use to get there.

Medication

Anxiolytics

The medication we usually think of for anxiety disorders are the anxiolytics, which are a class of sedative medications called benzodiazepines. Their calming effect comes by raising the level of the inhibitory neurotransmitter GABA in the brain. Benzos are meant to be a short term medication, while you build other anxiety management skills. The general rule is no longer than a year, and some prescribers will only prescribe them for a few months. While I have definitely known people on them for a long time, that is becoming increasingly rare since more and more prescribers are getting censured from their boards for doing so. They have side effects that include problems with balance, memory, and vision, and they increase drowsiness, which is great if you are trying to sleep but not great if you are trying to operate heavy machinery. Some people experience depressive symptoms on them as well.

They can also be habit-forming. There's an increasing epidemic of benzodiazepine misuse, federal data show U.S.

deaths associated with benzodiazepines increased from 135 in 1999 to 11,500 in 2017. Individuals at the FDA have said the number of individuals who were prescribed both opioids and benzodiazepines grew by 41% (2.5 million) between 2002 and 2014. This is important because while benzos can be fatal in and of themselves, overdose is typically caused in combination with opioids because the sedative effects of both exacerbate each other. "More than 30 percent of overdoses ascribed to the opioid crisis also involved benzodiazepines, and the population at the highest risk is individuals over 50.

I'm not saying all this to proclaim *"oooh scary, no take!"* but to reiterate these are strong medications with potentially serious consequences. And there are valid reasons for doctors being hesitant to prescribe them and/or continue to prescribe them over time. If you are on or looking to get on an anxiolytics, be prepared to have other active strategies in place so this isn't your long term anxiety management plan. While these medications are used relatively interchangeably, a list of the common ones and how they are typically prescribed is here.

Anxiolytics and How They Are Typically Prescribed

Anxiety Disorders	Alprazolam (Xanax)
	Chlordiazepoxide (Librium)
	Clorazepate (Tranxene)
	Diazepam (Valium)
	Lorazepam (Ativan)
	Midazolam (Versed)
Seizure Disorders	Clonazepam (Klonopin)
	Clorazepate (Tranxene)
	Lorazepam (Ativan)
	Clobazam (Onfi)
	Diazepam (Valium)
Insomnia or trouble sleeping	Estazolam (Prosom)
	Flurazepam (Dalmane)
	Quazepam (Doral)
	Temazepam (Restoril)
	Triazolam (Halcion)
Anesthesia Adjacent	Midazolam (Versed)
	Lorazepam (Ativan)
	Diazepam (Valium)
Muscle Relaxation	Diazepam (Valium)
Alcohol Withdrawal	Chlordiazepoxide (Librium)

Antidepressants

Antidepressant medications are also very commonly prescribed for anxiety disorders with the idea that the effect they have on neurotransmitters helps mitigate anxiety. Antidepressants take 4-6 weeks to produce noticeable effects, unlike anxiolytics which produce very quick relief. Probably the most typically used antidepressant for anxiety are the SSRIs, particularly Lexapro (escitalopram) and it's older form Celexa (citalopram). Tricyclics have been shown to be effective for most anxiety disorders, and MOAIs are used for panic disorders and social phobias more specifically.

Types of Prescription Antidepressants and Info on How They Work Best

The medications prescribed for depression are also the same medications commonly prescribed for anxiety disorders. And there is a lot of overwhelming and confusing information about the different classes of antidepressants. I've known tons of ridiculously smart people who had no idea what they were on, why they were on it, and what it was expected to do. That can lead to a helluva lot of problems.

So here is some basic info to get you started, with thanks to the Mayo Clinic and Aaron Sapp, MD, for the fact-checking and the reminders that what I see in my office as common isn't necessarily so common for the real world.

Medication Category	How We Think They Work	What We Worry About	Examples
Selective Serotonin Reuptake Inhibitors (SSRIs). Doctors often start by prescribing an SSRI. These medications generally cause fewer bothersome side effects and are less likely to cause problems at higher therapeutic doses than other types of antidepressants are.	SSRIs specifically affect serotonin levels by blocking the brain from recycling it (which is all reuptake means) during the neurotransmission process, leaving more serotonin available to combat depression.	The biggest issue I see complaints about is the sexual side effects. SSRIs can also affect sleep and increase irritability, agitation, and restlessness. Nausea and other common side effects are less likely to be long term, and may not be as bad with a different kind of SSRI since they all work a little differently.	• Fluoxetine (Prozac), • Paroxetine (Paxil, Pexeva) • Sertraline (Zoloft) • Citalopram (Celexa) • Escitalopram (Lexapro) • Vilazodone (Viibryd)
Serotonin and Norepinephrine Reuptake Inhibitors (SNRIs). SNRIs help relieve both common and less common symptoms of depression. Sadness, irritability, and long term chronic nerve pain are all targeted by SNRIs.	SNRIs block the recycling (reuptake) of both serotonin and norepinephrine, leaving more of both available to combat depression.	Side effects of SNRIs are pretty similar to those of SSRIs.	• Duloxetine (Cymbalta) • Venlafaxine (Effexor XR) • Desvenlafaxine (Pristiq, Khedezla) • Levomilnacipran (Fetzima)

Medication Category	How We Think They Work	What We Worry About	Examples
Atypicals (Which only means the antidepressant catch-all category.)	This category includes several common antidepressants that don't fit well in one of the other categories but are thought to change levels of dopamine, serotonin and/or norepinephrine.	Side effects will all differ, obviously. Though it is important to note here that bupropion is the one antidepressant that does not have sexual side effects (though it does make you more susceptible to seizures, so it's not necessarily the magical wonder drug of the bunch).	• Bupropion (Wellbutrin/ Zyban, Forfivo XL, Aplenzin) • Mirtazapine (Remeron) • Nefazodone • Trazodone • Vortioxetine (Brintellix)
Other Medications (Not Necessarily Antidepressants)	A prescriber may want to consider other medications in support of managing depression, including mood stabilizers, ADHD medications, anti-anxiety medications, medications for alertness, etc. Feel free to ask "Why this one specifically? What are you hoping to accomplish by having me take this?"	Varies	Varies

Medication Category	How We Think They Work	What We Worry About	Examples
RARELY PRESCRIBED *Monoamine Oxidase Inhibitors (MAOIs).*	These medications prevent an enzyme called monoamine oxidase from removing neurotransmitters associated with mood (norepinephrine, serotonin and dopamine from the brain) with the idea that they will then operate at proper levels, alleviating depression.	You have to maintain a really strict diet, because MAOIs can interact with certain foods, herbal supplements, and medications to the point of causing very high blood pressure. So these medications are typically used when other ones have failed.	• Isocarboxazid (Marplan) • Phenelzine (Nardil) • Selegiline (Emsam) • Tranylcypromine (Parnate)
RARELY PRESCRIBED *Tricyclic Antidepressants (TCAs).* TCAs tend to cause more side effects than newer antidepressants, so they generally aren't prescribed unless you've tried other antidepressants first without improvement.	TCAs block the reabsorption (reuptake) of both serotonin and norepinephrine, leaving more of both available to combat depression.	TCAs block other chemical messengers in the body (not just serotonin and norepinephrine) so they are associated with more side effects than SSRIs and SRNIs, including tremors, excessive sleepiness, blood pressure issues, and weight issues.	• Imipramine (Tofranil) • Nortriptyline (Pamelor) • Amitriptyline • Doxepin • Desipramine (Norpramin) • Amoxapine • Protriptyline (Vivactil) • Trimipramine (Surmontil) • Maprotiline

Other Medications That Your Prescriber May Recommend

Buspirone (Bupspar) is another medication that is used for both short-term anxiety and long-lasting anxiety disorders

Like antidepressants, it takes several weeks to be fully effective because it is also a serotonin receptor agonist. Common side effects can include dizziness, headaches, nausea, and trouble sleeping or weird dreams.

Beta-blockers are often treated for heart conditions, because they block (makes sense) the release of the stress hormones adrenaline and noradrenaline in certain parts of the body. They are used to treat heart conditions because they reduce the force with which blood is pumped through your body. Since high blood pressure is a common physical symptom of anxiety, especially social anxiety, they are sometimes prescribed for them as well. A beta-blocker such as propranolol (Inderal) can help with specific situations that trigger anxiety like giving a presentation at work or school. To help reduce your anxiety symptoms in stressful situations, such as attending a party or giving a speech. The side effects that may occur are the same as the ones mentioned above for buspirone plus possible dry mouth and shortness of breath.

Other Complementary Therapies

So here is where we talk about the treatments that our ancestors used and used effectively that were then tossed aside when modern medicine came along with its pills and surgeries. What used to be our first course of treatment now has gotten a bad rap as woo-woo bullshit. And it's entirely legit to not want to spend your hard-earned money and even harder-earned free time fucking around with woo-woo bullshit. But a lot of the things that have gotten a bad rap actually have a lot of research backing up their efficacy, even if, because they don't benefit the pharmaceutical industry, they are generally discredited and not covered by insurance.

And many of them can be used either alone or with Western practices (like traditional talk therapy or allopathic meds). Like naturopathic treatments, these are things that are designed to encourage the body's own capacity to heal and self-regulate—to keep the funnel wide enough to manage life stressors without collapsing in with an ever-narrowing perspective and ability to manage life.

One of the biggest supporters of complementary therapies (at least in my hood) is the Veterans Administration. We have a program in town that provides massage, acupuncture, reiki, and EFT (more on all of those below) to local veterans. Our local VA has noticed that the people who do that work also do far better with their VA providers in therapy, med management, and symptom reduction. They actively recommend complementary therapies *and* have been training their own people in some of these therapies. As an example, some of their MDs are now also using acupuncture in the clinic.

Y'all. If the military-industrial complex thinks reiki works, it might just mean that reiki fucking *works*. So here is my list of complementary treatments that I encourage, have experience with, and have found the research behind. It's not a complete list (and I would actually love to hear if you have any additions you think I should consider).

Acupuncture/Acupressure/EFT

Acupressure and acupuncture use the same principles, but **acupuncture** involves using the actual needles in the skin while **acupressure** involves the tapping of certain points instead of breaking the skin.

However, whether tapping or using needles, it works by stimulating certain points on the body to promote healing and/or reduce pain. What is really interesting is that as we learn more about the vagus nerve system, we are seeing lots of commonality in modern nerve mapping and five-thousand-year-old acupuncture charts. The vagus nerve is large and complex. Though it's a cranial nerve, it wanders down throughout the body to many other organs, sending messages back to the brain. Recent research (led by Stephen Porges) demonstrates that the vagus nerve plays a huge role in managing our social behaviors and responses to stress and trauma. Mood disorders (like other mental health issues) have a whole-body response to what is being fired off in the brain.

Acupuncture and acupressure meridians follow both vagus nerve maps and then even deeper through the fascia that runs throughout our bodies.

If you are interested in a combo deal of acupressure with talk therapy, some therapists use Emotional Freedom Technique (EFT), which includes acupressure and self-talk strategies. The EFT is something you do yourself, with guidance from the practitioner, using the same main activation points an acupuncturist would (bonus if people touching you squicks you out). The self-talk helps you reframe the stories your brain has been telling you while creating new ones in the process. There are tons of free videos that walk you through the basic process, though a therapist will help you modify the scripts to work through your specific situation.

Biofeedback/Neurofeedback/Alpha-Stim Treatment

Biofeedback is the electronic monitoring of all bodily functions, which helps people learn to control responses that were previously automatic. **Neurofeedback** focuses specifically on the brain signals with the same intent: to help individuals learn to manage their brain responses.

We have far more control over our body and brain's responses than we realize, and both bio and neuro can be great ways to augment or even speed up our unfuckening by giving us immediate feedback when our brain and body start to get into fight, flight, and freeze mode. You essentially play a video game with your brain. It sounds as Tron as all fuck, but you are set up with a Pac-Man type game, or something similar, which you can only complete when you keep your brain waves in the optimal zone for your wellness. We know that so much of depression is caused by brain misfiring. Neurofeedback can help you intentionally reshape how the brain fires messages to mitigate this response.

I also include **Alpha-Stim** treatment in this section, since even though it is a passive treatment, it falls under the same principles. Alpha-Stims are designed to increase alpha brain waves (which are the great combination of calm and alert that we all crave). It works like neurofeedback except the machine does the work for you rather than you training that brain state yourself. You hook up the machine to your earlobes and turn it on, and it does the brain wave-changing work for you. Alpha-Stims have lots of research demonstrating that they help with sleep, pain, anxiety, and a host of other conditions. I do use an Alpha-Stim in my practice, especially when clients are working through a trauma narrative that is important to them but causing a lot of pain. The Alpha-Stim can really help them recover faster from one of those tough therapy days! I have also had clients use them to improve symptoms in their daily lives without other medications. Alpha-Stims have to be purchased with a prescription in the U.S., but any counselor can prescribe them like I do, not just a medical doctor.

Chiropractic Treatment

What? Chiropractic care for mental health issues? Isn't that for bad backs? Beyond, again, the fact that depression can manifest as physical pain, chiropractic is a holistic form of treatment that operates from the idea that adjustments of the spine and body can facilitate nervous system support. Pain and nervous system support? Totally huge parts of a trauma reaction for many people, which can be the genesis of depression. And sometimes these physical symptoms are far worse than the emotional ones. Many chiropractors (as well as massage therapists and acupuncturists) build nutritional assistance into their work as well.

Energy Healing (Reflexology/Reiki)

Energy healing is one of those things that seemed super weird, even for me, for many years. Then I read more about it, and tried it for myself, and *wow*.

So, **energy healing** is based on the idea that our bodies operate on all these frequencies that we can tap into to promote our healing. Weird? Not so much. One study showed energy healing being as effective as physical therapy. UCLA now has a whole fucking *lab* that studies electrical activity in the body. And UCLA is a state-funded school. Tax money invested in energy healing: that's some serious street cred.

Reflexology focuses on applying pressure to areas of the ears, hands, and feet, with the idea that these areas are connected to other points throughout the body (and polyvagal theory bears this out). **Reiki** (a Japanese term for guided life force energy) is the channeling of energy from a practitioner (or from one's own self) into the person who needs healing in order to activate the body's own healing process. These forms of energy healing (among others) help us find the stuck points in the body where we tend to hold our trauma in order to better release them.

And by the way, acupressure (tapping work like the EFT I talked about) is considered a form of energy healing as well as a variation on acupuncture.

Massage

Everyone knows what massage is, I don't have to explain it, but people are surprised when I suggest it as healing for emotional issues, not just physical pain. First of all, physical pain can absolutely be a symptom of emotional health issues. But even if that isn't going on, massage can be a safe way for people to learn to relax and feel comfortable in their skin.

So many times after a trauma we feel disconnected from our bodies. We hold so much of what we term "mental health issues" in our physical bodies. The point of massage is the ability to ground yourself back into your body. This helps us recognize and catch our symptoms earlier on in the depression funnel and makes it far easier to prevent a full relapse.

I realize massage can be very triggering for certain types of trauma. Definitely don't force yourself out of your comfort zone. Some people are way more comfortable with a pedicure and a foot massage than with a full body massage. Some people prefer a hot bath or hot tub soak rather than having someone's hands on their skin. Anything that feels safe for you while helping you reconnect with your physical body can really help you manage your emotional health, not just the pain associated with it.

Weighted Blankets

You may have heard of weighted blankets for helping to manage anxiety or soothe an individual on the autism spectrum. They also really support sleep and depression recovery. The pressure of the blanket engages the nervous system and helps the body to re-regulate in general. Weighted blankets are usually made with plastic pellets (which makes the blankets machine washable and not as hot as, say, a heavy wool blanket).

In terms of weight, for adults, look for a blanket that is about 10% of your ideal body weight, and for kids and teens it will be about 10% of their weight plus a pound or two. An occupational therapist can help you figure out exactly the right formula for you if you're unsure. A weighted blanket is something else I keep at my office for people to try out and see if they like it and is the thing that people end up loving and going out and buying more than any of my other therapy hacks.

Natural Supports

Natural Supports are the people who love you just because you belong to them. Your family, your friends, teachers, coworkers, and others who go above and beyond their role in your life to support you getting better. Having people who love us just because they *do* is so, so, so important to getting better.

I understand that you may not have supportive people in your life, or your anxiety may be lying about which people care and want to see you better. If people offer support, lean into the discomfort of trusting that they mean it. If they ask to help, let them!

If you don't have people, it's time to find your people. Actively searching out friends when you already feel like shit is really difficult. Maybe start small and online, finding groups on social media where you can reach out to others with mental health issues, like the Facebook group for the Icarus Project. Maybe you can find a local support group. But honestly? It doesn't have to be a group of people who are also struggle with anxiety. . . you can look for folks who also like movies, or reading, or hiking, or picking up and putting down heavy things. Getting out and exploring can be of great benefit to your healing, and bonus is you might meet some not-shitty humans.

It takes far more strength to accept help than reject. Be strong enough to allow others into your life and show you they care about you.

Peer Supports

There is a huge body of research that shows that peer-to-peer support partners (as the Substance Abuse and Mental Health Administration [SAMHSA] refers to them as) are an enormous part of many peoples' wellness and recovery processes. This makes sense. Someone who has similar lived experience has a level of empathy, understanding, and compassion that other people don't. There are phenomenally caring treatment providers out there, but we often connect most to the people who have also traveled the same path we are on.

There are lots of names for this role in communities, including: recovery coach, sponsor, family partner, and systems navigator, to name a few. You will generally find these folks in recovery organizations (twelve-step or otherwise), community mental health clinics, and the like. There are also clinical professionals with lived experience who may share that experience as part of the work they do with people. If peer supports are available wherever you are seeking treatment, give it a try. Someone who has been in the same hole you are in is sometimes the best person to talk to about finding the way out, yanno?

Finding Treatment Providers

No matter what treatment strategies you are researching, there is a decent chance you are looking for a treatment provider in that area. Whether it is a prescriber, a professional counselor, an occupational therapist to help you find the best weighted blanket, or a nutritionist to help you adjust your diet and add some supplements.

Lifestyle, medical model, or complementary strategies all have experts that may help your journey. But I swear, some days it feels like 99.44% of the battle is finding a provider who you can get in to see in a reasonable amount of time, really listens, is competent in treating you, and is a real partner in helping you get better.

You may be getting treatment in a community mental health setting, where you don't have much choice in providers, but if you do have choices, finding people who you really connect to and can work well with is important. So here are some things to consider asking when researching:

What is their license and/or certification? Where did they train? Who provides their practice oversight?

Why these questions are important: If the person is a licensed doctor or therapist or something, it's pretty obvious, but there are some service providers that may have exceptional training but not be licensed for any number of reasons. For example, less than half of the states in the U.S. have a process for naturopathic doctors to become licensed. This doesn't mean that NDs working in states that do not provide licensing for them are suddenly poorly trained and incapable of doing their job. Even something as unregulated as reiki has training programs with a lineage that you can ask about. Asking these questions can help you weed out the sketch-ass people who have a PhD from an online diploma mill with no accreditation from the people who really know their shit.

What do they specialize in? What is their treatment approach? What is their training in your specialty areas?

Why these questions are important: I've seen so many people list specialties in which they had no real training or experience. That's setting everyone up for failure. It also could be that they specialize in a certain method of treatment that isn't what you are looking for even if they have *tons* of experience and training. My treatment approach is pretty eclectic, so when people call me looking for a very structured treatment plan, I send them to someone who is great at that. I may have the training they are looking for, but not utilize that training in a way they would expect.

What is your experience in treating [insert your personal treatment needs]? Are you comfortable with working with [insert your issues]?

Why these questions are important: It gives you an idea of their ability to spitball when things go awry (and let's face it, most of us aren't gonna have every need met with a cookbook approach). It also may be that they don't have much experience with your issue but are willing to learn and are open to the challenge. And if they are someone you feel comfortable with and y'all work well as a team, that's okay. I have zero problem as a provider saying, "I have no idea, let me do some research and ask in my consulting group and look for some options for that issue."

These are other circumstances I have that could impact my care: [lay them all on the line]. Are you comfortable dealing with these issues?

Why these questions are important: Some providers won't or can't work around all the stuff you have going on in your life, and it's better to know that right away. There may be stuff going on that makes working with a provider a deal-breaker. If you have other confounding medical issues. If you have other confounding mental health issues. If you are needing an assessment or diagnosis for other care or to receive benefits. If you are court involved and need the provider's testimony.

What do you charge? Are there additional fees for other services? How do you accept payment? Do you take insurance? Do you take HSA cards? Will you give me a superbill for reimbursement?

Why these questions are important: I try to give lots of information about my fees and options surrounding them. Not all providers (or their staff) think to do this, so it's really important that you ask. Especially if you are paying out of pocket and are having to budget and plan for your services . . . then, for example, you find out there is an additional fee for the diagnosis letter you were needing. Been there personally, and it really sucks.

Are you comfortable working with my other providers?

Why this question is important: Because they may *need* to be in contact with your other providers. For example, if I am providing nutritional support to someone who is on prescription medications, I may need to chat with the prescribing docs about what I am wanting to treat and why. But sometimes it isn't even that complicated, and we just need to share info to better help our shared client. You want providers willing to do the legwork and pick up the phone and talk to the other people who are treating you.

Questions to Ask Your Prescriber About Medications and Supplements

- What symptoms does this medication or supplement treat?

- How does it work in the body?

- Is this intended for short or long term use?

- If it is for short term use what will be our longer term treatment plan?

- What side effects could I have from this medication or supplement?

- How long will they probably last?

- What side effects are dangerous? Which mean I should go to an emergency room? Which should I notify you about and how do you want to be notified?

- How should I notify you if I want to discuss discontinuing this medication or supplement?

- If I no longer want to take this medication will I need to taper off of it?

- How long will it take to start working?

- Does this medication interact with any other drugs I'm taking?

- Does this medication interact with any other supplements or herbs?

- What else do you recommend for me to consider in order to help with my symptoms?

Longer-Term Self-Training

Whether you are in a place where you can't access therapy at this time, don't want to go to therapy, or have a great one that you work with regularly, a lot of your anxiety treatment will be self-propelled. Meaning you are going to be working on this shit in your regular life all the time (therapists call this "homework") . So these are some of the techniques you can start working with to help better manage your anxiety.

Learned Optimism

Like all other brain retraining, there are certain things that can really help combat chronic anxiety. It isn't a magic bullet, better-immediately type cure, but the idea of training yourself to be optimistic has some merit behind it. There is a guy named Martin Seligman who is a legit big deal in my field. He was studying learned helplessness when he noticed that there are certain qualities that those obnoxiously, cheerful Susie-Sunshine optimistic people generally have:

Permanence: Optimistic people don't dwell on bad events, and approach them as temporary setbacks. If they get neg'd on, they bounce back more quickly. They also believe that good things happen for reasons that are permanent. Essentially, the world is fundamentally in their favor.

Pervasiveness: People who are happy monkeys tend to keep failure in its proper place. They recognize failure in one area as only belonging in *that* area, rather than meaning they are a failure at *all the things all the time*. They also tend to let the things they are good at inform the rest of their lives, rather than keeping that in its own space. Sucking at basketball doesn't mean you will now make a shitty risotto. And if your risotto rocks, it is an indicator that *you* rock. And that you should cook more often. And invite me for dinner, I love risotto.

Personalization: Our cheerful buds blame bad events on bad circumstances rather than bad selfhood, but take good circumstances as indications that they are good people. So basically failures are events, not people. But successes are people, not events. If you dig me?

Interested in figuring out which way you wire? You can take the Learned Optimism test online if you;re interested.

Understanding what makes an optimist gave Seligman an idea. If we can learn helplessness and pessimism, then why can't we learn optimism and a positive outlook? Especially if we know the three big indicators we are shooting for? Let's start with challenging our Neg Gremlins.

[h3]Take Action: Challenge Your Neg Gremlins

Seligman created an **ABCDE** model designed to help you reframe your thinking as optimistic. And yes, it looks a ton like Albert Ellis' Rational Emotional Behavior Therapy (REBT) and Aaron Beck's Cognitive Behavior Therapy (CBT). We all borrow from each other's shit all the time. Therapists and researchers are assholes like that.

Think about the last time you felt anxious and write down some notes for each of these five letters:

Adversity. What bullshit is going down that generally triggers your anxiety response?

Belief. What are your beliefs about this event? Be honest, if your anxiety is triggered a lot, you are probably running a thought pattern in the direction of *"this situation is fucked!"* Beliefs just mean your thoughts, how you interpret what happened. Not your emotional responses. It may also be a flash of a memory, rather than a fully-formed thought, if the situation triggered a trauma response.

Consequences, though really it should stand for Cookie. Seligman didn't agree with me that once you think that shit's fucked you should go have a cookie. Instead, he wants you to look at how you reacted to the situation and to your beliefs. This is where your emotional responses (how you felt) go, as well as what you did/how you behaved.

Disputation. This is where you literally argue with the neg-gremlins your brain is throwing down and focus your attention on a new way of coping. Create a new story to use instead.

Energization. What was the outcome of focusing your attention on a different way of reacting? Even if you were still pretty anxious, did you handle the situation better than you may have in the past? Over time, with doing this, do you notice that your anxiety is starting to fizzle out *finally*?

To start with, just fill out the first three categories (A-B-C). Think back and look for examples of pessimism and negativity. Highlight those instances. Did you beat yourself up way more than you expected?

Give it a few days to sink in and then sit down with this list again and add the last categories (A-B-C-D-E). This is gonna be harder—this is active work to challenge that pessimism and teach yourself optimism instead. But you got this, rock star. It takes practice, so stick with it!

1. **Adversity:** Just the facts, baby. Describe what happened (who, what, where, when) being as precise and detailed as you can.

2. **Beliefs:** What were you thinking? Like, exactly. What was your self-talk? Don't care if it was crude, ugly, or weird. Write it down. If it sparked a memory or flashback, that counts, too!

3. **Consequences:** How did these thoughts affect how you felt? How you behaved? What went on in your body? What emotions did you experience? How did you react?

4. **Dispute:** There are four different ways you can dispute these negative beliefs:

a. Evidence? Is there evidence that your belief is based in reality? If someone says "I hate you," then the belief that they hate you has some evidence behind it, right? But most beliefs really don't.

b. Alternatives? Is there another way you can look at this situation? What were the non-static circumstances (you don't always bomb a test, so maybe you were overtired from being sick)? What are the specifics (sucking at basketball doesn't make you a lame human being or even a lame athlete)? What did others contribute to the situation (is it really *all* your fault???)?

c. Implications? Okay, so maybe you fucked up. Is it really a total catastrophe? What's some perspective you can add (If I failed in that job interview . . . that doesn't mean no one will hire me from now to infinity)?

d. Usefulness? Just because something is true doesn't make it useful. How can you frame the experience as one that gives meaning to your life? Do you have a better respect for those things or people you value? Can you better demonstrate that respect now?

5. Energization: How do you feel post-disputation? Did your behavior change? Your feelings? Did you notice

anything within the problem that you didn't notice before? Maybe even created a solution?

Now go celebrate your success here, hot stuff! By doing this work on yourself, you start extinguishing anxiety as your go-to response because you don't see the world around you as so much of a threat.

That's not bad, eh?

Cognitive Defusion: Turning Off the Judgement Machine

One of the best tools from Acceptance and Commitment Therapy reframes our emotional responses through a technique called defusion. Defusion is the process of recognizing our thoughts and feelings as something we have rather than something that we are. Let's try it with some of the main meta-messages you have held about yourself:

• My mind tells me I am too much of . . .

• My mind tells me I am not enough of . . .

• My mind tells me I do too much of . . .

• My mind tells me I do not do enough of . . .

• My mind tells me I lack . . .

Now take this list and sit with it for a half a minute or so as something you are.

- I am too awkward.

- I am too lazy.

- I don't move fast enough.

Check in with yourself. How do you feel in your body after just half a minute of taking ownership of these thoughts?

Now try a shift out of judgement, by labeling it as a thought that exists, not something that you are.

- "I'm noticing that I'm having a thought about being too awkward.

- "I'm noticing that I am having a thought about being lazy.

- "I'm noticing that I am having a thought that I do not move fast enough."

All defusion means (and yeah, sorry for the term . . . we like to create words for concepts to confuse as many people as possible) is that you are separating your self-ness out of your thoughts and noticing them as something that exists rather than something you are.

Check in with yourself again. How does your body feel when you are no longer fused with these thoughts as indicative of your self-hood?

Embracing Challenge Stress Through Mindset Training

The author of the book *The Upside of Stress*, Kelly McGonigal (whose research became the starting point for a lot of what I write about here) states: *"Embracing stress is a radical act of self trust."*

We've been told not to though, haven't we? We're told to avoid stress, to calm down, that it isn't good for us. Research bears this out. Harvard Business School professor Alison Wood Brooks asked hundreds of people if they are anxious about a big presentation, what's a better way of handling it: feel excited or try to calm down. 91% of people said "try to calm down." Although, as mentioned eleventy times above, the stress isn't in and of itself bad.

A 2013 Harvard study found that just saying *"I'm excited"* out loud can reappraise stress as excitement . . . it's easier for the brain to jump from anxious feelings to excited ones rather than calm ones. Cortisol is activated and you can consciously label it as excited instead of stressed, which changes your experience. One of the biggest predictors of stress overwhelm is our perception of not being up to the task, so focusing on the fact that we are, indeed, up to it shifts our thinking.

The term *mindset* is one of those words we associate with those performance coach guru types. Tony Robbins isn't wrong, though. Mindsets are really nothing more than the beliefs we have about ourselves and the world that shape our realities.

Mindset training has a direct impact on our stress response. A stronger physical stress response was associated with higher test scores . . . for people who have had mindset training. Another study demonstrated that just by telling people *"You're the kind of person whose performance improves under pressure"* increases their task performance by 33%.

And yes, individuals with anxiety can absolutely benefit from mindset training. Since stress is one of the biggest anxiety triggers, researchers have demonstrated that the stress response (at least the beginnings of it) is the same for people who have anxiety and those who do not. It's our perception of what it means that differs. Disrupting that stress response can end up circumventing anxiety and panic attacks. Jeremey Jamison's Social Stress Test experiment found that people with social anxiety had just as much benefit from mindset training than people who didn't struggle with anxiety.

Salvatore Maddi termed this mindset building a form of *hardiness* . . . meaning the courage to grow from stress. This is how someone can be "good at stress" . . . it doesn't mean that difficulties don't get to us and stress doesn't bother us, but we value growth, accomplishment, and being an active participant in our own lives enough that we befriend our stress response when we can and learn from it when it overwhelms.

Any stressful situation can become an opportunity to practice a mindset shift. When you notice your stress response activating, you can remind yourself that your body is reacting to something *because it's important to you.* Then use that energy to help carry you through the situation. Whether you are getting through a stressful interview or fighting facism, being alert and engaged and present is vital to success.

Mindset training seems awkward at first, but once you build that neural pathway it becomes more natural and more likely to be your automatic response . . . you won't have to work so hard at it over time. Your stress mindset will also change how you react to others' stress. Mindset leads to resilience and motional resilience is one of the first lines of defense against mental illnesses like anxiety.

Mindset Training: Having a GOOD Mindset

You can also practice mindset training as part of your daily self-care routine. I like the GOOD acronym of mindset training since it doesn't involve any kind of fake hype about shitty situations, it really just is about grounded in your own self-efficacy. I mean, if you are reading this your survival rate thus far is 100%, right?

Gratitude—Focusing on gratitude is a really good part of our mental health in general and becomes a perspective shift in our day. This doesn't mean discounting what's problematic, but focusing on what's good in your life helps you do the next part more easily. And that's . . .

Openness to Possibilities—If we are gratitude-focused we are far more likely to be aware of solutions, support, and opportunities around us. In a negative mindset we are far more likely to dismiss things that are available to us (or not notice them at all) because we are overwhelmed and frustrated with life in general.

Opportunities In This Experience—This means no matter what experience wo are having, we are focusing on the opportunities we can find within them. We can learn more about different situations and ourselves even if we don't achieve the success we were hoping for. As someone who does a lot of political advocacy work, I can tell you that every lost battle taught me a new strategy of approach for next time.

Determine—Visualize yourself embracing the challenges ahead successfully. This is just hardiness in action. If you plan for your success you are in the right frame of mind to tackle the project. And no, you aren't more frustrated if things don't go perfectly. I've found that I'm more proud of myself for going in prepared and positive because I feel like I really gave it my all.

More Shit that Helps
Deep Breathing

When I work with kids I call it belly breathing. When I work with vets, police officers, and first responders I call it tactical breathing. The official term is diaphragmatic breathing or abdominal breathing which are just the most ridiculous words ever . . . I swear to Buddha, we must make this shit up just to see if we can get people to follow along.

So if you have seen any of those terms it's totally all the same thing. And all it really means is that you are taking in your breaths by contracting your diaphragm, which is a muscle that lies horizontally across your body, between your abdominal cavity and your thoracic cavity.

Sounds complicated? Not so much. You totally know how to take a deep breath. It's when your belly moves instead of your chest. You get far more oxygen in your blood when you are breathing in this manner, which will disrupt the anxiety response. Have you ever been so anxious that you felt light headed and about to pass out? Your breathing was likely totally to blame. You weren't breathing in a way that gave you the oxygen you need to manage your anxiety response.

If you want to practice this, lie down and put something on your belly. Your favorite stuffed animal, your unopened growler bottle, whatever. You should see it move while you breathe.

Yup, that's it, you got it.

Try to focus on your breathing instead of the other bullshit chatter that your brain is insisting you pay attention to. Counting helps, too. Try these counts for breathing in, holding, and breathing out.

Only count as high as you can comfortably go. You aren't gonna get graded on your breathing and it isn't meant to be stressful. If you're asthmatic, have allergies, etc., anything more than 6 seconds may be literally impossible. No sweat, okay?

Breathe In and Count To	Hold and Count To	Breathe Out and Count To
3	3	3
3	3	6
6	6	6
6	6	9
9	9	9
9	9	12
12	12	12

Passive Progressive Relaxation

Now we are going to work on relaxing each part of your body moving progressively down. This isn't one of those exercises where you tense up first so you can then relax yourself and feel the difference. That's a useful exercise on other occasions, but not when you already fucking know you are tense and don't need anything else making you more tense.

If it helps you to have prompts, you can find lots of guided progressive relaxation exercises on YouTube.

Start with the deep breathing. You know how to do this part now, so you can move the teddy bear or growler. Lie down, relax, and lay your arms and hands, palms to the earth, down to your side next to you. Close your eyes if that feels safe and comfortable for you.

- Start at the top of your head. Tune in, beginning with your crown, moving slowly down your scalp. Feel your ears relax.

- Feel your temples relax, and then your brows.

- Feel your eyes relax, then your cheeks, then your nose, and then your mouth. Relax your lips and your tongue.

- Feel your throat relax. Then your neck.

- Feel your shoulders relax. Focus on letting them drop everything they've been holding for you. They get to rest, too.

- Focus on your right hand. Let the calm flow from your right shoulder, down your arm. Through your wrists, then into each finger. Start with your thumb and move through each finger to your pinky, relaxing every digit.

- Now focus on your left hand. Let the calm flow from your left shoulder, down your arm. Through your wrists, then into each finger. Start with your thumb and move through each finger to your pinky.

- Now focus back on your shoulders, and let the relaxation flow through your chest down into your belly. Your belly is moving gently as you continue deep breathing, but otherwise has no other work to do right now. It doesn't have to hold itself up or in with any tightness.

- Go back up to your shoulders, and let the relaxation flow down your upper back to your lower back. You've been holding a lot there, haven't you? Maybe the entirety of the world. You don't have to, at least for right now. Let it go for a while.

- Relax through your buttocks, through your root chakra, and down through your hips. Let the calm flow down through your thighs.

- Move down to your knees, then your calves.

- Move down to your ankles. Your feet. Let yourself relax each toe. Start with your big toe and move to your pinky toe.

Once you feel ready, open your eyes and slowly get back up again. You may feel a little sleepy, or woozy, or fuzzy. That's okay. Take your time rejoining the world and remember what relaxed feels like. You're allowed to feel that way!

Mindfulness Meditation

No saffron robes needed, I promise. But meditation releases dopamine, serotonin, oxytocin, *and* endorphins. And it's cheaper than Crossfit. 3000 years of Buddhist practice has something going for it, yeah?

Here's my recipe for mindfulness meditation:

Sit upright. If you can do this without back support, like on the floor on a cushion then good on you. If you need a straight back chair, do that. If you can't sit at all, that's okay, too. Get yourself in whatever position is most comfortable. The reason sitting is better than laying down is that the point is to fall awake, not fall asleep. But the point is also to not be in screaming fucking pain, so don't stress it.

Soft-focus your eyes so they aren't closed but they are seeing without actually seeing. You know what I mean. Be visually spaced out because what you are really going to be paying attention to is inside you.

And now you are going to breathe in and out. And focus on your breath. If you have never done this before it's going to be weird and hard. But for the record, if you have done this a zillion times chances are still good that it will be weird and hard.

If you catch yourself being distracted, just label it "thinking" and go back to focusing on your breath. Thinking isn't a failure in the least. It's gonna happen. And noticing it and bringing the mind back to the present moment is the point. So it's a total win.

Treat your bodily reactions like any other random thought. Itching is common. If you catch yourself itching, label it thinking three times before succumbing to the urge to scratch. You may be surprised at how often your brain is creating things for you to focus on. Of course, if you have real pain, don't ever ignore that. Rearrange yourself for comfort and don't be a hero.

A lot of people feel awful during meditation, thinking they suck at it because they are continuously distracted by chatting thoughts. That's okay. Your brain is desperately seeking to story-tell. All kinds of distracting stuff is going to come up. You are going to think about what you need to cook for dinner. Or a conversation you had at work. Or whether or not you should buy new sneakers or go to a movie this weekend.

I'm not even going to pretend that this shit is easy to do when you are spun up. But it's important to at least try. Because part of a panic attack is the stories our brain starts telling us about the attack itself. And it's generally not a pretty story. The chemicals released during an anxiety or panic attack are designed to get your breathing ramped up and your heart racing. So your brain starts insisting that you are going to have a heart attack or will stop breathing. That's not going to happen. When you catch that thinking, remind yourself that's a biochemical response, but not reality.

And here is the thing about mindfulness meditation . . . research shows that it disrupts the storytelling process of the default network. We used to think the only way to do that was a distraction by outside events and stimulus, but the opposite works, too.

So keep breathing. The continued, conscious effort to breathe and un-tense will slow the heart rate back down and help you get more oxygen flowing. It's a literal chemical counter-balance. And it gives your brain the space it needs to tell itself new stories.

When Someone You Love Has Anxiety

This can be tough, right? Even if you have anxiety yourself and you totally get it. When you are relying on someone but they are all up in their struggles and can't be there for you. When you don't know what the fuck is going on, just that they are checked out.

It's okay to ask, it's okay to talk about it, and it's okay to be there for them in whatever ways works for y'all.

Say, "Hey what's up. I haven't seen you in a while (or plans were canceled, etc.). Do I have halitosis you aren't telling me about or did I piss you off without intending to? I know your anxiety can be bad sometimes and I was wondering if that was something you were struggling with and if so I'm available to talk about it/not talk about it/help in any way I can."

It's okay to be upset if their anxiety is fucking over your plans, too. But own it for exactly that. Your friend already feels shitty enough. So say, "Yeah, I was bummed that you didn't show up last night. I love spending time with you. If your anxiety is that bad right now, should we try for different kinds of plans? Or do you need to tell me when you want to do stuff so you don't feel pressured to hang out when you really don't want to?" This can get more difficult if it is someone you live with. A partner, roommate bestie, or family member. Y'all are both miserable with how anxiety is affecting your lives continuously because you share space.

But no matter what the nature of the relationship, it's important to support people without taking over their lives. Asking *What would be helpful right now?* can be a very illuminating question. Maybe they would really love an accountability partner to go walking with. Or maybe looking for a therapist feels like an overwhelming task but they are completely willing to go.

The important thing is to not work harder for someone than they are working for themselves. I have had family members reach out to me wanting to schedule an appointment for someone they love and my first question is always "Do they know you are doing this?" If the answer is yes, they are helping them sort through some overwhelm to get to therapy and that's great. If the answer is "no" . . . they just have a plan on dragging an unwilling grown-ass human to my office and I won't book the appointment until that grown-ass human is on board and willing to be there.

Having good boundaries in all relationships is always better for everyone involved, and it may be the one thing that saves the relationship when someone is really struggling with their mental health. The answer to "What would be helpful right now?" may not be something you can carry for them and it is always better to express that with love rather than doing it anyway and months down the line expressing it with great resentment.

Conclusion

So what do we do with all this? Do these coping skills make anxiety all magically, immediately better?

Of course not. And anyone who offers a super quick cure in that regard is an epically shitty, false-hope peddler. Without understanding what's happening, anxiety is just an epically shitty experience followed up by a mindless attempt at treatment.

But now you have a new weapon: The "why."

Your brain is busting its ass to protect you and keep you safe. It's just gone off the rails out-of-control in trying to figure out what to protect you from. And it's impossible to control something we don't understand. The why things are happening part helps make the fixing it part actually work. That's been my experience. And the experience of most everyone who I've ever talked to about anxiety. Likely your experience, too.

Anxiety is a motherfucker. I'm not about to lie to you in that regard. All the things that make us brilliantly, wonderfully, amazingly human are the exact same things that make us prone to this diffuse, unpindownable sense of anxiety and dread. And the world we live in is a bubbling cauldron of shit to be anxious about.

But when it comes down to it, the existentialists like May and Kierkegaard were right. The more we are able to fight for ourselves, for our unique humanity and individual reasons for being, the more we win. And the more the anxiety inside us settles down. And the more the anxiety that surrounds us doesn't consume us. We have to fight for ourselves and fight for the people we love.

We have to do it even when we are anxious.

Fucking hell, especially then.

All these skills, all these ways of supporting your struggles with anxiety? Think of them as your personal rebel alliance fighting for your right to survive. There will never be anything else you do that is more radical than investing in your own self-worth and self-care.

A COUPLE OF THE BOOKS I SHOUTED-OUT HEREIN

Why Zebras Don't Get Ulcers by Robert Sapolsky

This book is totally about the body as a biological machine and explains why humans are more susceptible to stress-related diseases (like, you know, anxiety) than animals are. The last chapter is more self-help oriented. But if you like to nerd out on the science part, this book is the schizz (Sapolsky is also heavily featured in the National Geographic documentary Stress: Portrait of a Killer. Last time I looked, it was up on YouTube.)

The Meaning of Anxiety by Rollo May

May was smart AF, y'all. And an amazing philosopher as well as a clinician. I think he missed out on many of the ways lack of privilege can affect anxiety but it doesn't mean that many of his ideas weren't brilliant and a good starting place. And hey, he was a well-educated, well off white dude in the middle 20th century, so not exactly an intersectional feminist (and, TBF, relational cultural theory didn't even *exist* yet) so I give him a pass on that end. It's still a good grounding if you are interested in the historical underpinnings of anxiety.

Toward a New Psychology of Women by Jean Baker Miller

Jean Baker Miller's theories about mental health looked at how stereotypes have shaped mental illness. She took what all of the institutional ideas about power, success, strength, and autonomy really mean and turned them on their head.

In a Different Voice by Carol Gilligan

Gillian's work molded neatly with that of Miller's even though they were not working together at the time they were researching and writing these books. Gilligan was focused on looking at human development through a new lens, instead of only the current theories available regarding mental health. Her interest was in the space that lies between experience and thought, and how those things shape and inform each other. Her use of the word "voice" to replace the notion of "selfhood" is something that I have carried forward in my own research.

Learned Optimism by Martin Seligman

If we can learn helplessness, we can learn the reverse, right? Fuck yeah, that's right! Human beings are wired to the negative as a protective mechanism that doesn't serve us super well in the long run. Seligman uses classic cognitive therapy techniques with a twist to show people how to rewire their brains into more positive thinking and responses.

Furiously Happy: A Funny Book About Horrible Things by Jenny Lawson

Jenny Lawson (The Bloggess) writes about surviving the whole host of disorders she has struggled with, including depression and anxiety. She walks that balance of not taking it all so seriously and taking it *very very* seriously. It's a fine line, isn't it? She does the thing. This makes it possible to laugh and relate and actually feel better without disrespecting the seriousness of what you're going through.

Some of My Other Favorite Books On The Topic

First We Make The Beast Beautiful by Sarah Wilson

Sarah Wilson's personal journey with anxiety led her to do tons of research and interviews and share the things that she has found the most helpful. Like Jenny Lawson, Sarah writes her reality with no filters so you can see the good, bad, and ugly.

The Upside of Stress by Kelly McGonigal

The stress cycle in and of itself is not a bad thing. This book shows all the research in how the perception of stress feeds our response to it and the impact it has on our bodies.

Burnout by Emily Nagoski and Amelia Nagosoki

This book is specific to the stress cycle and overwhelm experienced by women in this culture, some of which I touched on in this book. This book uses a lot of science and empathy to help you understand and work through your biological stress cycle, plus tips on tapping out from cultural standards (such as needing to have a perfect body) that make all of these issues worse.

The Gift of Fear (And Other Survival Signals That Protect Us From Violence) by Gavin de Becker

Hear me out. I want you to have a life with as little anxiety as possible. But I want you to experience fear as a very real emotion that you should listen to and respond to. Gavin de Becker writes about how we ignore those very important bodily signals that something is not right and covers the science of how fear works and why we should pay heed to it.

Notes on a Nervous Planet by Matt Haig

I consider this book the Rollo May of the 21st century, it really speaks to how society feeds anxiety which we always, always, always need to take into account when working through our own issues. The personal is political and the political is personal.

REFERENCES

10 lesser-known symptoms of anxiety that you should know about—Ewen's Room: Promoting Wellbeing & Mental Health. (2020, November 14). Retrieved December 17, 2020, from ewensroom.com/10-lesser-known-symptoms-of-anxiety-that-you-should-know-about/

Advisory Board Daily Briefing. (2019, August 21). The drug epidemic that's largely flown under the radar. Retrieved January 07, 2021, from advisory.com/en/daily-briefing/2019/08/21/benzodiazepines

Alsene, K., Deckert, J., Sand, P. et al. Association Between A2a Receptor Gene Polymorphisms and Caffeine-Induced Anxiety. Neuropsychopharmacol 28, 1694–1702 (2003). doi.org/10.1038/sj.npp.1300232

Audiffren, M., & André, N. (2019). The exercise–cognition relationship: A virtuous circle. Journal of Sport and Health Science, 8(4), 339-347. doi:10.1016/j.jshs.2019.03.001

Bahrami, F., & Yousefi, N. (2011). Females are more anxious than males: a metacognitive perspective. Iranian journal of psychiatry and behavioral sciences, 5(2), 83–90.

Bandelow, B., Michaelis, S., & Wedekind, D. (2017). Treatment of anxiety disorders. Dialogues in clinical neuroscience, 19(2), 93–107. doi.org/10.31887/DCNS.2017.19.2/bbandelow

Baran, S.E., Charles E. Armstrong, Danielle C. Niren, Jeffery J. Hanna, Cheryl D. Conrad,

Chronic stress and sex differences on the recall of fear conditioning and extinction,

Neurobiology of Learning and Memory, Volume 91, Issue 3, 2009, Pages 323-332,

ISSN 1074-7427, doi.org/10.1016/j.nlm.2008.11.005.

Barahmand U. Meta-cognitive profiles in anxiety disorders. Psychiatry Res. 2009 Oct 30;169(3):240-3. doi: 10.1016/j.psychres.2008.06.029. Epub 2009 Sep 6. PMID: 19733915.

Beckwith, N., McDowell, M. J., Reisner, S. L., Zaslow, S., Weiss, R. D., Mayer, K. H., & Keuroghlian, A. S. (2019). Psychiatric Epidemiology of Transgender and Nonbinary Adult Patients at an Urban Health Center. LGBT health, 6(2), 51–61. doi.org/10.1089/lgbt.2018.0136

Benzodiazepines Drug Class: Side Effects, Types & Uses. (n.d.). Retrieved January 07, 2021, from rxlist.com/benzodiazepines/drug-class.htm

Bostwick, W. B., Boyd, C. J., Hughes, T. L., & McCabe, S. E. (2010). Dimensions of sexual orientation and the prevalence of mood and anxiety disorders in the United States. American journal of public health, 100(3), 468–475. doi.org/10.2105/AJPH.2008.152942

Bouman, W. P., Claes, L., Brewin, N., Crawford, J. R., Millet, N., Fernandez-Aranda, F. & Arcelus, J. (2017). Transgender and anxiety: A comparative study between transgender people and the general population. International Journal of Transgenderism, 18 (1), pp.16-26.

Blackledge, J. T., & Hayes, S. C. (2001). Emotion regulation in acceptance and commitment therapy. Journal of clinical psychology, 57(2), 243–255. doi.org/10.1002/1097-4679(200102)57.2<243::aid-jclp9>3.0.co;2-x

Brellenthin, A. G., Crombie, K. M., Hillard, C. J., & Koltyn, K. F. (2017). Endocannabinoid and Mood Responses to Exercise in Adults with Varying Activity Levels. Medicine and science in sports and exercise, 49(8), 1688–1696. doi.org/10.1249/MSS.0000000000001276

Callinan, S. Johnson, D., & Wells, A. (2015). A Randomised Controlled Study of the Effects of the Attention Training Technique on Traumatic Stress Symptoms, Emotional Attention Set Shifting and Flexibility. Cognitive Therapy and Research, 39(1), 4-13.

Cavanagh M & Franklin J (2000). Attention Training and hypochondriasis: Preliminary results of a controlled treatment trial. Paper presented at the World Congress of Cognitive and Behavioral Therapy, Vancouver, Canada.

Callesen, P., Reeves, D., Heal, C. et al. Metacognitive Therapy versus Cognitive Behaviour Therapy in Adults with Major Depression: A Parallel Single-Blind Randomised Trial. Sci Rep 10, 7878 (2020). doi.org/10.1038/s41598-020-64577-1

Cheng, L., Pan, G. F., Sun, X. B., Huang, Y. X., Peng, Y. S., & Zhou, L. Y. (2013). Evaluation of anxiolytic like effect of aqueous extract of asparagus stem in mice. Evidence-based complementary and alternative medicine : eCAM, 2013, 587260. doi.org/10.1155/2013/587260

Facts & Statistics. (n.d.). Retrieved December 17, 2020, from adaa.org/about-adaa/press-room/facts-statistics

Fenske JN, Petersen K. Obsessive-Compulsive Disorder: Diagnosis and Management. Am Fam Physician. 2015 Nov 15;92(10):896-903.

Fergus, T.A., Bardeen, J.R. (2016). The Attention Training Technique: A Review of a Neurobehavioural Therapy for Emotional Disorders.Cognitive and Behavioral Practice, 23(4), 502-516.

Fergus, T.A., Wheless, N.E., & Wright, L.C. (2014). The attention training technique, self-focused attention, and anxiety: A laboratory-based component study. Behaviour Research and Therapy. 61, 150-155.

Freeman, Z. (2019, July 21). Panic Attacks and Anxiety Episodes Linked to Vitamin Deficiencies in Groundbreaking Study. Retrieved December 17, 2020, from healthy-holistic-living.com/panic-attacks-and-anxiety-episodes-linked-to-vitamin-deficiencies-in-groundbreaking-study/?utm_source=HHL

Goodwin G. M. (2015). The overlap between anxiety, depression, and obsessive-compulsive disorder. Dialogues in clinical neuroscience, 17(3), 249–260. doi.org/10.31887/DCNS.2015.17.3/ggoodwin

Hilimire, M. R., DeVylder, J. E., & Forestell, C. A. (2015). Fermented foods, neuroticism, and social anxiety: An interaction model. *Psychiatry research*, *228*(2), 203–208. doi.org/10.1016/j.psychres.2015.04.023

Hofmann, S. G., & Hinton, D. E. (2014). Cross-cultural aspects of anxiety disorders. Current psychiatry reports, 16(6), 450. doi.org/10.1007/s11920-014-0450-3

Jacka, F. N., Pasco, J. A., Mykletun, A., Williams, L. J., Hodge, A. M., O'reilly, S. L., . . . Berk, M. (2010). Association of Western and Traditional Diets With Depression and Anxiety in Women. American Journal of Psychiatry, 167(3), 305-311. doi:10.1176/appi.ajp.2009.09060881

JAMA and Archives Journals. "Anxiety Disorders Linked To Physical Conditions." ScienceDaily. ScienceDaily, 24 October 2006. <sciencedaily.com/releases/2006/10/061024010331.htm>.

Jones, K. H., Jones, P. A., Middleton, R. M., Ford, D. V., Tuite-Dalton, K., Lockhart-Jones, H., Peng, J., Lyons, R. A., John, A., & Noble, J. G. (2014). Physical disability, anxiety and depression in people with MS: an internet-based survey via the UK MS Register. *PloS one*, *9*(8), e104604. doi.org/10.1371/journal.pone.0104604

Kiecolt-Glaser, J. K., Belury, M. A., Andridge, R., Malarkey, W. B., & Glaser, R. (2011). Omega-3 supplementation lowers inflammation and anxiety in medical students: a randomized controlled trial. Brain, behavior, and immunity, 25(8), 1725–1734. doi.org/10.1016/j.bbi.2011.07.229

Keynote Address to the Fifteenth Focusing International Conference 2003 in Germany, & Hendricks-Gendlin, M. (n.d.). Focusing as a Force for Peace: The Revolutionary Pause. Retrieved January 08, 2021, from focusing.org/social-issues/hendricks-peace

Kleinknecht, R. A. (2002). Mastering anxiety: The nature and treatment of anxious conditions. Cambridge, MA: Perseus Pub.

Knowles, M. M., Foden, P., El-Deredy, W. and Wells, A. (2016), A Systematic Review of Efficacy of the Attention Training Technique in Clinical and Nonclinical Samples. Journal of Clinical Psychology, 72(10), 999–1025.

Kohrman-Glaser, L., & Kohrman-Glaser, L. (2014, November 17). Emotion, Brain, & Behavior Laboratory. Retrieved December 23, 2020, from sites.tufts.edu/emotiononthebrain/2014/11/17/are-you-anxious-that-ocd-is-no-longer-an-anxiety-disorder-a-rational-behind-the-resent-change/

Koopman C, Classen C, Cardeï¿½a E, Spiegel D: When disaster strikes, acute stress disorder may follow. J Trauma Stress 1995; 8:29–46Crossref, Medline, Google Scholar

Lago, T. R., Hsiung, A., Leitner, B. P., Duckworth, C. J., Balderston, N. L., Chen, K. Y., Grillon, C., & Ernst, M. (2019). Exercise modulates the interaction between cognition and anxiety in humans. Cognition & emotion, 33(4), 863–870. doi.org/10.1080/02699931.2018.1500445

Lebrón K, Milad MR, Quirk GJ. Delayed recall of fear extinction in rats with lesions of ventral medial prefrontal cortex. Learn Mem. 2004 Sep-Oct;11(5):544-8. doi: 10.1101/lm.78604. PMID: 15466306.

Letamendi, A. M., Ayers, C. R., Ruberg, J. L., Singley, D. B., Wilson, J., Chavira, D., Palinkas, L., & Wetherell, J. L. (2013). Illness conceptualizations among older rural Mexican-Americans with anxiety and depression. *Journal of cross-cultural gerontology*, *28*(4), 421–433. doi.org/10.1007/s10823-013-9211-8

Levauz, M.N., Laroi, F., Offerlin-Meyer, I., Danion, J.M., Van der Linden, M. (2011). The Effectiveness of the Attention Training Technique in Reducing Intrusive Thoughts in Schizophrenia: A Case Study. Clinical Case Studies. 10(6), 466-484.

Millet,N., Julia Longworth & Jon Arcelus (2016): Prevalence of anxiety

symptoms and disorders in the transgender population: A systematic review of the literature, International Journal of Transgenderism

McLaughlin, K. A., & Hatzenbuehler, M. L. (2009). Stressful life events, anxiety sensitivity, and internalizing symptoms in adolescents. Journal of abnormal psychology, 118(3), 659–669. doi.org/10.1037/a0016499Merrill, A. (n.d.). Anxiety and Autism Spectrum Disorders. Retrieved January 05, 2021, from iidc.indiana.edu/irca/articles/anxiety-and-autism-spectrum-disorders.html

Moritz, S., Wess, N., Treszl, A. Jelinek, L. (2011). The Attention Training Technique as an Attempt to Decrease Intrusive Thoughts in Obsessive–Compulsive Disorder (OCD): From Cognitive Theory to Practice and Back. Journal of Contemporary Psychotherapy. 41(3), 135-143

Murray, J., Theakston, A., & Wells, A. (2016). Can the attention training technique turn one marshmallow into two? Improving children's ability to delay gratification. Behaviour Research and Therapy, 77, 34-39.

Nassif, Y. & Wells, A. (2014), Attention Training Reduces Intrusive Thoughts Cued by a Narrative of Stressful Life Events: A Controlled Study. J. Clin. Psychol., 70, 510–517.

National Institute on Drug Abuse. (2020, November 16). Benzodiazepines and Opioids. Retrieved January 07, 2021, from drugabuse.gov/drug-topics/opioids/benzodiazepines-opioids

Neurotypical vs Neurodivergent: What's the Difference? (n.d.). Retrieved December 23, 2020, from daivergent.com/blog/neurotypical-vs-neurodivergent

Norrholm, S. D., & Ressler, K. J. (2009). Genetics of anxiety and trauma-related disorders. Neuroscience, 164(1), 272–287. doi.org/10.1016/j.neuroscience.2009.06.036

Normann, N., & Morina, N. (2018). The Efficacy of Metacognitive Therapy: A Systematic Review and Meta-Analysis. *Frontiers in psychology*, *9*, 2211. doi.org/10.3389/fpsyg.2018.02211

Obsessive-Compulsive Disorder, 2014-09-01Z, Volume 37, Issue 3, Pages 257-267, Copyright © 2014 Elsevier Inc.

Otte C. (2011). Cognitive behavioral therapy in anxiety disorders: current state of the evidence. Dialogues in clinical neuroscience, 13(4), 413–421. doi.org/10.31887/DCNS.2011.13.4/cotte

Papageorgiou C. & Wells A (1998). Effects of attention training on hypochondriasis: a brief case series. Psychological Medicine, 28, 193-200.

Papageorgiou C & Wells, A (2000). Treatment of recurrent major depression with attention training. Cognitive and Behavioral Practice, 7, 407-413.

Psychiatry.org. (2017). What Are Anxiety Disorders. Retrieved December 17, 2020, from psychiatry.org/patients-families/anxiety-disorders/what-are-anxiety-disorders

Rosenwohl-Mack A, Tamar-Mattis S, Baratz AB, Dalke KB, Ittelson A, Zieselmar et al. (2020) A national study on the physical and mental health of intersex adul the U.S. PLoS ONE 15(10): e0240088. doi.org/10.1371/journal.pone.0240088

Russell, S. T., & Fish, J. N. (2016). Mental Health in Lesbian, Gay, Bisexual, and Transgender (LGBT) Youth. Annual review of clinical psychology, 12, 465–487. doi. org/10.1146/annurev-clinpsy-021815-093153

salehi A, Baghban I, Bahrami F, Ahmadi A. The Effect of Emotion Regulation Training based on Dialectical Behavior Therapy and Gross Process Model on Symptoms of Emotional Problems, Zahedan J Res Med Sci. 2012 ; 14(2):e93581.

Sartori, S. B., Whittle, N., Hetzenauer, A., & Singewald, N. (2012). Magnesium deficiency induces anxiety and HPA axis dysregulation: modulation by therapeutic drug treatment. Neuropharmacology, 62(1), 304–312. doi.org/10.1016/j. neuropharm.2011.07.027

Schwartz, Jeffrey M., et al. "Systematic Changes in Cerebral Glucose Metabolic Rate After Successful Behavior Modification Treatment of Obsessive-Compulsive Disorder." Archives of General Psychiatry 53.2 (1996): 109-13. ProQuest. Web. 14 Nov. 2014.

Schoenfeld, T. J. Pedro Rada, Pedro R. Pieruzzini, Brian Hsueh, Elizabeth Gould. Physical Exercise Prevents Stress-Induced Activation of Granule Neurons and Enhances Local Inhibitory Mechanisms in the Dentate Gyrus, Journal of Neuroscience 1 May 2013, 33 (18) 7770-7777; DOI: 10.1523/JNEUROSCI.5352-12.2013

Snyder, H., Kaiser, R., Warren, S., & Heller, W. (2014). Obsessive-Compulsive Disorder Is Associated With Broad Impairments in Executive Function A Meta-Analysis. Clinical Psychological Science. Retrieved November 15, 2014, from cpx.sagepub. com/content/early/2014/07/16/2167702614534210.full

Stein, D., Fineberg, N., Bienvenu, O., Denys, D., Lochner, C., Nestadt, G., Phillips, K. (2010). Should OCD be classified as an anxiety disorder in DSM-V? Depression and Anxiety, (27), 495-506. Retrieved November 16, 2014, from dsm5.org/Research/ Documents/Stein_OCD.pdf

Sharpe, L., Nicholson Perry, K., Rogers, P., Dear, B.F., Nicholas, M.K., Refshauge, K. (2010). A comparison of the effect of attention training and relaxation on responses to pain. PAIN, 150(3), 469-476.

Siegle, G.J., Ghinassi, F., Thase, M.E. (2008). Neurobehavioral therapies in the 21st century: summary of an emerging field and an extended example of cognitive control training for depression. Cognitive Therapy and Research, 31, 235-262.

Shin, L., Liberzon, I. The Neurocircuitry of Fear, Stress, and Anxiety Disorders. Neuropsychopharmacol 35, 169–191 (2010). doi.org/10.1038/npp.2009.83Social Anxiety Disorder: More Than Just Shyness. (n.d.). Retrieved December 14, 2020, from nimh.nih.gov/health/publications/social-anxiety-disorder-more-than-just-shyness/index.shtml

Stress Symptoms: Physical Effects of Stress on the Body. (2019, August 01). Retrieved December 17, 2020, from webmd.com/balance/stress-management/stress-symptoms-effects_of-stress-on-the-body

Team, F. (2020, August 21). Is a Hidden Medical Condition Causing Your Anxiety? Retrieved December 23, 2020, from health.clevelandclinic.org/is-a-hidden-medical-condition-causing-your-anxiety/

ɔrabi, M., Kesmati, M., Harooni, H. E., & Varzi, H. N. (2013). Effects of nano and ʌventional zinc oxide on anxiety-like behavior in male rats. Indian journal of rmacology, 45(5), 508–512. doi.org/10.4103/0253-7613.117784

Valmaggia, L., Bouman, T.K. & Schuurman, L. (2007). Attention Training with auditory hallucinations: A case study. Cognitive and Behavioral Practice, 14, 127-133.

What Are Anxiety Disorders? (n.d.). Retrieved December 14, 2020, from psychiatry. org/patients-families/anxiety-disorders/what-are-anxiety-disorders

What's Normal and What's Not? (n.d.). Retrieved December 23, 2020, from adaa. org/understanding-anxiety/obsessive-compulsive-disorder/just-for-teens/whats-normal-whats-not

Wells, A. (1990). Panic disorder in association with relaxation induced anxiety: An attentional training approach to treatment. Behavior Therapy, 21, 273-280

Wells, A. (2007). The Attention Training Technique: Theory, effects and a metacognitive hypothesis on auditory hallucinations. Cognitive and Behavioral Practice, 14, 134-138.

Wells, A. (2009). Metacognitive therapy for anxiety and depression. New York: Guilford Press. (Contains the ATT treatment manual for therapists).

Wells, A. White, J. & Carter, K. (1997). Attention Training: Effects on anxiety and beliefs in panic and social phobia. Clinical Psychology and Psychotherapy, 4, 226-232.

Wells A. Meta-cognition and worry; a cognitive model of generalized anxiety disorder. Behav Cogn Psychoter. 1995;23:301–20.

Wells A. Cognitive Therapy of Anxiety Disorders; A practice manual and conceptual Guide. Chichester: Wiley; 1997.

Williams, M. T., Chapman, L. K., Wong, J., & Turkheimer, E. (2012). The role of ethnic identity in symptoms of anxiety and depression in African Americans. *Psychiatry research*, *199*(1), 31–36. doi.org/10.1016/j.psychres.2012.03.049

Yazici, K., Pata, O., Yazici, A., Aktaş, A., Tot, S., & Kanik, A. (2003). Menopozda hormon yerine koyma sağaltiminin anksiyete ve depresyon belirtilerine etkisi [The effects of hormone replacement therapy in menopause on symptoms of anxiety and depression]. *Turk psikiyatri dergisi = Turkish journal of psychiatry*, *14*(2), 101–105.

Yule, M. A., Brotto, L. A., & Gorzalka, B. B. (2013). Mental health and interpersonal functioning in self-identified asexual men and women. Psychology and Sexuality, 4(2), 136-151. doi:10.1080/19419899.2013.77416

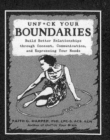